Ramiz Daniz

Expedition to India discovers Brazil

Baku -2022

Preface: - Associate Member of the Academy of Science,
Academician Ramiz Mammadov

Scientific editor: - professor Abbas Seyidov

Reviewer: - Doctor of geography Shamil Azizov
- Doctor of technical sciences Nugay Aliyev

Computer design: - Sinay Gasimova

Computer designer: - Sevinj Akchurina

Translator   - Hokume Hebibova

Ramiz Daniz *"Expedition to India discovers Brazil"*. **156 p.** **2022.**

Thus, real discovery of Brazil may be made clear. The expedition had to be started in 1493. Probably, preparation works were realized out of the Pyrenean peninsula and in Madeira Islands. As hot days had passed and stormy weathers were characteristic for autumn of those latitudes, this work had to be carried out on the north-western coast of Africa. They had to use other islands in order to prevent risks. From this standpoint, the most convenient geographical location was the location of Green Cape Islands and remote western point of Africa located near the Gulf of Guinea.

Portugal, which didn't want to declare its regard for the mentioned division, began to declare dissatisfaction after a year and demanded the Pope to move the demarcation line for 270 liq towards the west. Representatives of both kingdoms met with the participation of Alexander VI in Tordesillas in 1494 and the demarcation line was moved for 370 liq away from Azores (for 2200 km towards the west from those islands) according to the next treaty concluded on June 7. According to the treaty of Tordesillas, all territories located in the east of the demarcation line belonged to Portugal, but lands located in the west belonged to Spain.

The writer, researcher and publicist Ramiz Daniz was born in Baku in 1965. He graduated from secondary school in 1983. He has been a President grant holder since 2009 and he is a laureate of the *"Golden pen"* (2005) award. He is member of The Union of Azerbaijan Writers (1999) and Geography Society (2013).

He was winner of the international award instituted by the International Writers Union on 3 nominations in 2020 and Grand-Prix winner of the international award in 2021.

Preface
Expedition to India discovers Brazil

Scientists working in the field of history of geographical discoveries carry out some important works related discovery of America and create new scientific research works in order to elucidate this topical problem. Always difference of opinion occurs between scientists of this field and every created work has special significance in the field of geography. Ramiz Daniz has answered questions, which are interesting for scientists by discovering new facts at the result of his researches:

President grant holder on literature, laureate of the "Golden pen" award Ramiz Daniz writes literary works in several literary genres and scientific works.

Ramiz Deniz has been studying geographical discoveries and their history for 38 years, and writing fictional and scientific works at the same time. His works have been entered in the libraries in Paris, London, New York, Prague, Madrid, Moscow, Beijing, Tokyo, Madrid and many other cities. Total 357 books including translations have been published in Russian, English, German, Spanish, Italian, French, Portuguese, Polish and

Dutch by "AV Akademikerverlag", "Verlag Unser Wissen", "JustFiction Edition", "Lap Lambert publishing", "Scholars' Press", "Sciencia Scripts", "Palmarium Academic Publishing", "Our Knowledge Publishing", "Novas Edições Acadêmicas", «Edições Nosso Conhecimento», "Editions Notre Savoir", "Editions universitaires europeennes", "Edizioni Accademiche Italiane", "Sciencia Scripts", "Edizioni Sapienza", "Wydawnictwo Nasza Wiedza", "Editorial Akademica Espanola", "Wydawnictwo Bezkresy Wiedzy", "Ediciones Nuestro Conocimiento", "Qlobe Edit" publishing houses of Europe. Most of them are distributed by 14 large advertising companies in more than 50 foreign countries. Most works of the author "International science centre Maragino observatory", "Enigmatic discovery of Brazil", "Ambitions of Columbus and Vespucci's ruse", "King Manuel's plan and discovery of Brazil", "Admiral Piri Reis's map", "Transatlantic project of Columbus", "Brazil was opened in 1494", "Pope Alexander VI's demarcating line", "Letters, Paolo Toscanelli maps and Columbus calculations", "Rich financers, who defended Columbus's project", "Letters of Amerigo Vespucci compilation", "The largest Academy of

Sciences in the Middle Ages", "Columbus was aware of existence of America beforehand", "In XIII century, a famous scientist from Cordoba to Beijing", "500 years of America's discovery", "Christopher Columbus, Nasiraddin Tusi and discovery of America", "Pedro Cabral and Amerigo Vespucci`s travelling to the Brazilian coast", "The scientist passed ahead of centuries – Nasiraddin Tusi", "The development of geometry and mathematics at the Maragha Observatory", "Learning the secrets of Cosmos in ancient times", "Fernand Magellan's expedition and conquerors of three oceans", "Amerigo Vespucci, Martin Waldsemuller – secret bargain", "Nasiraddin Tusi and development of astronomy", attracted attention of the specialists.

Azerbaijan founds economical, cultural and political relations with other countries, integrates with the world and foreign countries are interested in science, education and culture of our country. That's why scientific research works of Ramiz Daniz may be interesting for scientists and ordinary readers, who learn the history of geographical discoveries. Probably he'll be invited to scientific conferences held abroad. Because Ramiz Daniz has found out many novelties and could deny most stereotypes.

Scientists of the world will learn that, the history of geographical discoveries is investigated in Azerbaijan too and they'll wait for next works of Ramiz Daniz.

Some obscure issues related the first travel of Christopher Columbus (1492-1493) including interesting facts about mysterious map used by him during the expedition are elucidated in **"Christopher Columbus, Nasiraddin Tusi and discovery of America"**. Unlike known main information, Ramiz Daniz writes that, Christopher Columbus knew where he had been going during his first transatlantic travel and could conceal it from the world community. As this fact is new, it is considered powerful pretension.

Real reasons of the failure of three Portuguese expeditions sent to the west of the Atlantic for research of America are explained in the work. The author prove by indicating perspicacity of Spanish monarchs and disbelief of the king of Portugal that *"Mathematical Union"* of Lisbon had significant role in appropriation of those territories by Spaniards.

Ramiz Daniz, who investigated scientific activity of the remarkable scientist of Azerbaijan Nasiraddin Tusi in

"The scientist passed ahead of centuries – Nasiraddin Tusi", discovered many facts in this field and elucidated worldwide essence of the scientist's most works.

The author mobilized all efforts and skills in order to investigate scientific services and achievements of well-known scientist of the East and discovered that some of his works have been stolen by other authors.

It is known that, Tusi had created masterpieces on astronomy, mathematics, geometry, ethics, played important role in development of these sciences and passed ahead of well-known scientists in these fields for some hundred years. The author recalled scientific works carried out by the most famous scientists of Greece, Ancient Rome, Byzantine, Egypt lived in ancient times and Muslim scientists of early middle ages in the field of geography, astronomy and mathematics, noted that, Nasiraddin Tusi had gained great achievements in mentioned fields and tried to emphasize his talent.

The astronomic catalogue **"Zij-i Ilkhani"** prepared by Nasiraddin Tusi was used in the discovery of America. Well-known astronomer Paolo Toscanelli and Columbus also benefited by this catalogue. Most scientists used this work of Nasiraddin Tusi for preparation of astronomic catalogues, Russian scientist Lobachevsky and other scientists of geometry benefited by **"Tahriru Uglidis"** and one copy of **"Shaklul Gita"** was published by German scientist Regimontan as his own work. One of teachers of I. Newton John Wallis played important role in popularization of N. Tusi in England as he used to read lectures based on **"Tahriru Uglidis"** in Oxford. Nicolaus Copernicus used the following theorem of Azerbaijani scientist proved in **"Memories of astronomy"** during preparation of **"The earth's revolution"**: "Two circles are on the same plane if the diameter of one circle is two times shorter that the diameter of the other one".

Investigation of the real author of the map prepared as though by Turkish admiral Piri Reis in 1513 and analyzed in most science centers of the world is very significant. After seven-year investigation, scientist of the USA Charles Hapgood found out that mentioned map had been prepared by someone, who knew spherical trigonometry. At that time, the person, who knew spherical trigonometry and applied trigonometry as an independent science, was Tusi.

The author discovered that, the map prepared with ancient manuscripts was constituted in Maraga observatory under the leadership of Nasiraddin Tusi. Besides it, he noted that, Christopher Columbus had sailed to coasts of the New World with that map and then Piri Reis owned that material together with the traveler's notes. In a word, America was theoretically discovered in Azerbaijan 200 years before the travel of Christopher Columbus and the author's purpose is to attract attention of scientists to this fact.

"Expedition to India discovers Brazil" concerns the problem, which make scientists of geographical discoveries to hesitate, and the author tries to prove that Brazil wasn't discovered by Pedro Cabral on April 22, 1500 by accident, it was discovered by Duarte Pereira in 1494 in accordance with secret agreement reached with the king of Portugal, but the result of that travel was kept secret for some reasons. In accordance with this work, though Spaniards firstly approached South America and Brazilian coasts, Portuguese were able to conceal them by means of the Pope and became owners of today's Brazil according to Tordesillas treaty concluded in 1494. Though Portuguese were agree to own lands located at 100 liq west of Azores in 1493, in accordance with the result of the secret expedition of Duarte Pacheco, who visited American coasts after a year, they appropriated large territories by moving the demarcation line between Spain and Portugal for 270 liq towards the west.

Vespucci didn't write anything about the expedition leader of his "third" travel G. Coelho in his letter and so, everybody thought that, the expedition was led by the Florentine accountant.

According to the information given by Vespucci, they had reached 32^0 southern latitude, sailed towards the southeast from there and reached 52^0 southern latitude. Why did they sail too far in the south? If Vespucci wouldn't return directly from 32^0 southern latitude, he could be satisfied with sailing down on the eastern coastline of the southern continent. It would be better as he would get opportunity to discover La Plata Gulf and the Strait of Magellan by sailing down towards 52^0 latitude on the eastern coast of the continent. It was impossible for him to reach the 52nd parallel of the southern hemi-sphere. Thus, this fact has been disproved. Vespucci noted that, the expedition sailed 7000 km towards the north for 33 days. How could the tired expedition overcome 7000 km with old vessels under the storms in 33 days?

The material including rich historical facts and some facts, which aren't noted in any scientific source, will certainly attract interest of the world's scientists and this discovery will have special significance. Very likely, the work will be discussed in Portugal, Spain and countries of the continent of America, the discovery of Brazil will be analyzed differently and some corrections will be made in the world's encyclopedia at the result of the objective decision.

These works may attract attention of intellectual readers of Azerbaijan and foreign countries, which are interested in scientific-literary heritage of scientists of the east and west including Nasiraddin Tusi, aren't indifferent to mysteries of travels of Christopher Columbus and Pedro Cabral and try to be far from illusions concerning discovery of America. Works, which are rich with sensetional information, will certainly be interesting for scientists of America and Europe and will start new course in the field of geographical discoveries. This field will be analyzed differently and books of Ramiz Daniz will be guide for scientists working in this field. Because the discovery of the continent of America and Brazil is the most interesting field of the history of geographical discoveries and mentioned works will be considered convenient source for investigation of this theme.

In general, it should be noted that, all three works are great present of Azerbaijan to the geography, so owing to them remarkable and well-known universities and unions of geography will acknowledge that, the history of geographical discoveries is investigated in Azerbaijan, which have ancient roots and rich culture as well.

There isn't any researcher working in this field of the geography in Azerbaijan. Ramiz Daniz is a pioneer of this field and I'm sure that, his works will be investigated at international institutes of geography and research centers together with works of Y. Svet, J. Baker, J. Beykless, M. Andre, Ch. Verlaine, I. Magidovich, V. Magidovich, V. Gulyayev, S. Morison, S. Swag and other researchers.

Ramiz Mammadov – Laureate of State Prize
Associate Member of the Academy of Science,
doctor of technical sciences, director of the Institute
of Geography of the Academy of Science

Cabral and Portugal kingdom demonstrating hegemony in the Atlantic Ocean

The Portugal kingdom, which desired to own most of lands in the Atlantic Ocean permanently, organized many sea expeditions in those areas. Most of those expeditions fulfilled tasks set under the secret gryphon in order to confuse foreign spies working on the territory of the kingdom. At the result of it, name of the real author of historically important discoveries became secret for the world community and absolutely fortuitous persons' names went down in history. But some adventurers used this opportunity and could adopt those mentionable successes. Sometimes very significant discovery may be showed as the success of quite different person in accordance with special order of the state leader. One of such unjust mission fell to the lot of the Portuguese sea traveler Pedro Alvaresh Cabral.

New gamble occurred in the history of geographical discoveries during last year of XV century. Large marine sailing towards the south and south-east (expedition (1500 members) consisting of 13 vessels (10 nau, 3 karavella), was considered one of large marines) lost its way in the ocean, sailed to the west and approached Brazilian coasts "by accident".

Of course, this thought is absurd. I want to note that, then Christopher Columbus had already discovered coasts of the New World, but nobody believed it. Because Columbus declared that, he had discovered the territory of the Eastern Asia. At the result of it, the discovery of world importance became the success of the adventurer by name Amerigo Vespucci. I descrybed this event in **"Coasts of the New World and ruse of Amerigo Vespucci".**

XV century should be analyzed in order to lay bare the truth. First of all, we have to investigate the leader of the expedition and his authority. Whom he was and why the business of state importance was entrusted him at the time when Spanish seamen competed with him in the Atlantic Ocean? It is interesting that though there was only one route, number of settings was two. And Pedro Cabral could overcome this work skillfully owing to experienced staff. Every leader has right to boast of such success.

The biography of Pedro Alvaresh Cabral (1467-1520), which was appointed the leader of the expedition, is very interesting.

Future commander born in 1467 at Belmonte castle, probably, in the family of nobleman began to work in the Kingdom Palace in accordance with the family tradition. His father was governor of Beyran Fernando Cabral and mother was Isabel Huveya. Pedro Huveya (he began to bear father's surname after death of his elder brother) moved to Lisbon when he was 11 and learned the literature, history, cosmography and military discipline there. King of Portugal Manuel I (1469-1521) accepted Cabral for the Kingdom Council and he was decorated with the Cross Order in the same year. At those days every nobleman couldn't achieve such successes. Vasco da Gama, who was very influential person, had introduced him as energetic, prompt and skilful administrator.

In accordance with some documents, Pedro Cabral was among noblemen when he was in North Africa and hadn't any naval experience. But in spite of it, he was entrusted with one of the largest expeditions consisting of 13 vessels. Well-known travelers as Bartolommeo Dias, Nicolau Coelho also were among members of the expedition and Cabral was protector of Don Manuel. He was entrusted with this position owing to the social position of his family and presentation of the father of his future wife Isabel Kashtru (they would be married after Cabral's travel to India) – Fernando de Noronha.

King Manuel I, who expected a lot from this mission, came to the port and presented the expedition and Cross flags to Cabral. Of course, it was great fame for the expedition leader. Some townsmen, who were aware of the king's coming, assembled in the port. During recent years several expeditions had started their travels from Lisbon in order to discover new lands. But Manuel I had visited none of them. His coming proved that Cabral's expedition was very significant. Cabral had to justify this trust.

Bishop of the city Diego de Ortiz blessed everybody at the religious ceremony took place before the travel.

In five days after vessels left Lisbon, the expedition passed Canary Islands and reached Green Cape Islands on March 22. The vessel of Vasco da Ataiden vanished at night between 22nd and 23rd March. After Green Cape Islands were left behind, Cabral changed course towards the south – to the Cape of Good Hope of Africa according to the instruction of Vasco da Gama and advices of Bartolommeo Dias. But the marine began to sail to the south-west without depending on them.

Portuguese met with strange event during the travel. They met with the land area (the territory of today's Porto Seguro located in Bahia) located on western coasts of the Atlantic Ocean on April 22 before reaching the Cape of Good Hope.

Portuguese marine travelling to India

The mission of Cabral was to break down resistance of inhabitants of India, to strengthen the influence of Portugal in those lands and to establish commercial relations. All these works had to be realized at peace. That's why more than 1500 people had been drawn into the travel. More than 1000 of them were fighters.

The staff of Cabral's expedition consisted of quite experienced and skilful seamen, which were participants of several previous travels. Boatswains were Bartolommeo Dias, who had discovered the south of Africa, Nicolau Coelho, who was participant of the first expedition travelled to India, and that expedition's annalist Duarte Pacheco Pereira. There was special staff for establishment of commercial relations with India.

Staff participated in the expedition proves that the purpose of the expedition wasn't to carry out exploration – it had political-diplomatic and commercial characteristics. Kinds of vessels (most of them were commercial), espesially the vessel of commercial representation of the king are obvious proofs of it, those vessels had to establish commercial relations with India. Their leader Ayres Correia was personal representative of the king and he had to use all efforts and skills in order to establish permanent commercial representation of Portugal in India. Even corresponding city had been chosen for this purpose – Europeans had to found factory in that city and Ayres Correia had to work as the secretary of the factory.

Copper, velvet, woolen clothes and other goods had been shipped on warehouses of vessels. Food had been stocked for a year and a half. Pero Vaz de Caminha, Arabian translator Al Masud (Monsaidi), who worked within the staff of Vasco da Gama, expedition's doctor, scientist, bachelor Juanish, eight Franciscan abbots working under the leadership of Enrique de Coimbra (he would work as a vicar in Calicut) and other religious employers had been attached to the secretary of the king in order to establish relations with Indian provinces in Calicut.

The expedition left the port of Lisbon on March 9, 1500. What was the task of the expedition, in general? Cabral had to maintain safety of vessels of Vasco da Gama, which had to travel to India and return to Portugal with valuable goods.

According to the plan, Cabral had to sail along the western coast of Africa 10^0 north latitude then he had to continue his travel towards the south-west in the open ocean.

This strange navigation course was chosen in order to maintain safety of the expedition, to save time and not to meet with unpleasant movements existing on coasts of the Gulf of Guinea.

Portuguese saw Brazilian coast on April 22, 1500 - on the holiday of Passover and so Brazil was discovered officially. But this discovery went down in history as an "accidental discovery". It's interesting that, Christopher Columbus also had mixed up that territory and Asia when he discovered the fourth continent in 1492.

May discoveries of world importance be accidental? After long researches, I came to the conclusion that expeditions having special missions meet with accidents during discoveries. Special tasks are given to leaders of expeditions before the travel and their real missions are kept secret.

Pero Vaz de Caminha noted in his letter addressed to the king Manuel I: "When we were at 660-670 liq away from San Nicolas Island of Green Cape Islands on April 21, we met with signs showing that coast isn't far from us as sargass, sedum and birds and saw land on April 22. Some participants of the expedition went ashore and met indigenous population. They were black and quite naked. They had bows and arrows..." According to the information given by Caminha, any serious conflict didn't occur between them and indigenous population. Nevertheless, armed conflict occurred when Vicente Pinson and Diego Lepe went ashore in Brazil. But Pedro Cabral's expedition didn't meet with such difficulty. According to received information, indigenous population helped Portuguese to cut trees. Flora and fauna of that land amazed everybody.

After 9 days - on May 1 - Friday Cabral decided to put wooden cross with slogan and emblem of the king of

Portugal on lands he had "discovered". Even abbot Enrique de Coimbra blessed everybody at the religious ceremony held with the participation of indigenous population.

On the same day Cabral sent Gaspar de Lemos to Lisbon with his vessel in order to inform the king about lands he had "discovered". He noted that, "discovered" territory would be called **True Cross Island (Vera Cruz)**. According to historical sources, that news didn't surprise Manuel I, though that "island" could be a stopping-place on the western way towards India. After some time, the king changed name of that territory, called it **"Santa Cruz" (Holy Cross)** and informed other monarchs of Europe about this fact.

Unlike expeditions of Pinson and Lepe, Cabral left some of his employees ashore. According to his order, two sea boys, who had been exiled and lived as deserters, were left ashore for ever.

The expedition left Brazilian coasts with 11 vessels on May 2, 1500 and according to the initial plan, went to the South of Africa and lost four vessels when passed the Cape of Good Hope. Unfortunately, Bartolommeo Dias, who had discovered the Cape of Good Hope in 1487, also was among dead travelers and his brother Diego

Dias was lost along Mozambique coasts. Lost Diego Dias discovered the largest island of Africa – Madagascar and later returned back safe and sound.

Large land area discovered by Cabral in the western coast of the Atlantic Ocean wasn't casual discovery, it was the greatest lie told by the Portugal Kingdom in XV century. It was impossible to lose way in the ocean, to sail thousands of kilometers blindfold with the expedition's marine, its staff, experienced navigators and captains. As all islands located in the Atlantic Ocean were unknown for inhabitants of the Old World, Cabral could discover the nearest unknown islands. Besides it, it must be noted that, Bartolommeo Dias, Nicolau Coelho and other professional seamen were among members of the expedition. I want also note that, the route for travelling from Lisbon to India was chosen by Bartolommeo Dias and Vasco da Gama. Vasco da Gama also used that route when he travelled to India 3 years before this event – in 1497. According to the instruction, Cabral had to pass unpleasant currents and to sail to the Indian Ocean without approaching the Cape of Storms located in the south of Africa.

The discovery full of enigmas

Most scientists, even the most famous scientists of geography, history of geographical discoveries and history accepted geographical discoveries without investigating some events concerning concrete discovery and such discoveries went down in history as "casual discoveries". "Casual" discovery of Brazil is obvious case of it.

They explained it as following: two strong currents moving towards west and northeast current existing on the territory between 10^0 north latitude and 10^0 south longitude. So vessels might sail to Brazilian coasts involuntarily under the influence of those natural calamities. Was such mistake possible, if Bartolommeo Dias, who could sail from Portugal to the south outskirts of Africa, participated in the expedition? Of course, it wasn't possible! If such serious mistake was made with participation of Dias, who knew eastern coasts of the Atlantic Ocean very well, how he could reach the Cape of Good Hope located at 10 thousand km away from Lisbon? So questions appear in accordance with that enigmatic discovery. One of main questions: might Pedro Cabral make that mistake and change the course according to the secret task of the king of Portugal Manuel I?

Scientists, who support the idea of "casual discovery", note that three strong currents existed in the middle of the Atlantic Ocean when Cabral sailed to the south. They write that, he had reached Brazilian coasts under the influence of those currents. First of all, let's analyze directions of mentioned currents.

The North Passat blows from east to west, the equatorial current moves from west to east and the South Passat blows from east to west. The Passat blowing from east to west has also to be mentioned. But in spite of it, scientists use this factor – currents moving towards the west and declare that, Pedro Cabral lost his way in the ocean and reached other place. But he might sail there purposely.

Even Duarte Pacheco Pereira could do it without Pedro Cabral's participation.

The leader of the expedition had to be experienced and skilful administrator, but not experienced seaman. He had to establish discipline among seamen and make even the most authoritative seamen to fulfil his tasks uncondi-tionally. Professional and authoritative seamen had to fulfil another task. It was the secret task given by the king Manuel I. The staff of the expedition had to prove existence of lands, which were located on western coasts of the Atlantic Ocean, were known by Portuguese and was secret for the world community.

As it was mentioned above, Vasco da Gama also could sail to Brazil under the influence of the equatorial current after changing the route before reaching the equator when sailed towards the south from the Atlantic Ocean in 1497.

If we investigate everything in strict succession, we can see that, there are a lot of obscurities in the discovery of Pedro Cabral. The expedition sailed directly towards the south after leaving San Nicolas Island – one of the central islands of the Green Cape Islands with 12 vessels on March 22. It continued travel towards the west after passing the equator and approached Brazilian coasts at 17^0 south latitude on April 22. San Nicolas Island is situated at 24^0 west longitude, Corumba Cape of Brazil is situated at 39^0 west longitude. It means that, the squadron had moved away from its southern line for 15^0 towards the west. It is equal to 1600 km at the latitude of Corumba Cape.

It wasn't possible to make such mistake at the time when the navigation had developed enough. Before this event Portuguese sea travelers, had discovered western coasts of Africa during several years, prepared map of those territories and presented it to the monarch of Portugal. Spanish spies observing Cabral's expedition, well-known navigators, boatswains and captains knew that, 1600 km couldn't be overcome blindfold after losing way in the ocean. Because vessels usually sail towards the west when there is South Passat. It doesn't make vessels to lose their ways. Portuguese changed their route purposely.

Pascual Mountain (536 m) discovered by Cabral is situated at 17^0 south latitude in the west of Corumba Cape and San Nicolas Island is situated at $16^0 \, 37^/$ north latitude.

I. P. Magidovich and V. I. Magidovich write that vessels had to sail $33^0 \, 30^/$ towards the latitude of Pascual Mountain and it was equal to about 3700 km.

According to information given by Pero Caminha, navigators had noted in their reports that they had overcome 4000 km. Then it isn't convincing that, Cabral changed the course directly towards the west after sailing 17^0 west latitude towards south.[1]

---

[1] И. П. Магидович, В. И. Магидович. Очерки по истории

So we may come to the following conclusion: the leader of the expedition wasn't Cabral at the ocean passage, it was managed by the seaman, who knew that route very well. Otherwise, seamen might meet with difficulties. Because when land isn't seen for a long time, members of the expedition rise in rebel, demand from admiral and captain to change the course.

The discover of Brazil was planned in Lisbon

The distance between San Nicolas Island and Corumba Cape (together with obstacles occurred in the ocean at the result of currents) is about 4000 km. Vessels sailed only with the south course. The distance was 1600 km at the latitude of Corumba Cape. It isn't convincing that, vessels lost their way at that latitude and sailed towards the west. Navigators had to understand such

географических открытий, II том. Москва, "Просвещение". 1982. стр. 54.

mistake. They had compass for manoeuvring in the ocean and determining orientation.

It is absurd to lose way when the compass is available. But it was possible from certain point of view at that time. It is possible to dodge from the fixed course when the weather is so foggy or windy, but this deviation may be 300-400 km or 500-700 km when storm is so heavy. According to diaries of the expedition, Portuguese didn't meet any serious natural calamity before passing the equator. It means that, it was impossible to lose way as the weather was good.

So Portuguese hadn't lost their way, they changed the course purposely and sailed to Brazilian coasts with fixed course and discovered mentioned lands. Marine of experienced navigators couldn't lose its way in the ocean for 1600 km.

As it was mentioned above, experienced captains and commanders as Bartolommeo Dias, Diego Dias, and Duarte Pacheco Pereira were participants of the expedition, these seamen noted the distance they had overcome on their diaries every day and controlled the course of vessels. So they had to understand that the expedition had dodged from the main course and warn Pedro Cabral. But it seems that, the leader of the expedition was satisfied with this deviation and he entrusted his assistants with the course at the ocean passage. In spite of it, the expedition dodged from the main course and sailed in other direction for a long time. But it isn't convincing argument.

It's necessary to analyze one important fact. The expedition lost its way in several days after moving away from Green Cape Islands. But Portuguese changed the course towards the Cape of Good Hope located in the south of Africa after leaving **"Vera-Crush"** "discovered" on May 2. Though they sailed 8000 km, didn't lose their way and reached the island soon. It means that, Portuguese navigators, who were very skilful in maneuvering in the open ocean, couldn't reach Brazilian coasts by dodging from the main course when sailed from Green Cape Islands to the Cape of Good Hope. If it happened – if the expedition lost its way and reached Brazilian coasts, it would lose its way when sailed to the Cape of Good Hope as Portuguese sea travelers used that route for the first time.

As it is known, Portuguese met with heavy storm when reached the south of Africa and lost four vessels together with their staffs. It should be especially noted that, Bartolommeo Dias, who had taken the expedition to the south of the Cape of Good Hope, also was the victim of that storm.

It should be noted that, it is possible to determine the geographical latitude continuously when the weather is enough good. How Portuguese could lose the way in that case?

Besides it, Cabral didn't punish any of his navigators or captains after understanding that the expedition is on the other side of the Atlantic Ocean. Nevertheless, such mistake shouldn't be forgiven at that time. Seamen were surprised. They knew that all tasks of their captains had been fulfilled professionally.

They began to explore the oast as soon as the land was seen. Besides it, Portuguese put big wooden cross on the coast instead of the stone emblem indicating that mentioned territory belonged to the Portugal Kingdom. What it was? It was next negligence or discovered lands weren't so significant? Nevertheless, every sea traveler had to approach such discovery seriously as Portuguese searched for lands on that part of the Atlantic Ocean for tens of years and couldn't achieve any success. Though Cabral achieved this "happiness", he was indifferent to his "discovery".

Why the expedition, which travelled from Lisbon to Calicut, chose strange course? Did Cabral know that other route had been chosen? Apparently, knew. That's why such negligence had to be punished by him. If that discovery wasn't important for Portuguese, why did Cabral send one of vessels, which had to sail to India to Lisbon in order to give information about the discovery? It is known that, ten days after the discovery of Brazil the leader of the expedition sent Gaspar de Lemos to Portugal with his vessel and the letter he had written. Information about the discovery was usually sent hastily when discovered geographical point had special importance. It means that, the discovery of Brazil had been planned beforehand and the world community had to be informed about it.

But who had to take the marine to Brazilian coasts, Bartolommeo Dias, who knew half of the way or other person who knew that route very well?

Vicente Janez Pinson, Diego Lepe or who officially discovered Brazil for the first time?

King Manuel I, who attached special importance to expeditions in the Atlantic Ocean, knew that, leaders of previous expeditions were experienced and skilful navigators and captains. So he couldn't entrust inexperienced person with the "discovery" of Brazil. The king had two purposes in sending Cabral's expedition to the Atlantic Ocean: to send marine under the leadership of the person, who knew the way to the Indian Ocean and to discover Brazil with the help of the seaman who knew certain part of coasts of South America.

What was the reason of such hastiness? Since 1500, Spanish travelers began to leave the Caribbean Sea and explore the territory of the continent located in the south.

N. S. Constantinova wrote: "After Portuguese received news that, Pinson approached Brazilian coasts on January 20 and Lepe did it on February 16, additional task also was given to the expedition".[1]

---

[1] Константинова Н. С. Путешествие в прошлое. Навигационная ошибка или секретная миссия?// Латинская Америка, № 5, M.2000, C.8.)

I want to elucidate route of expeditions travelled to Brazilian coasts. Parallels and meridians are the focus of attention. Tordesillas treaty had been concluded and borders had to be fixed.

Vicente Janez Pinson: Vicente Janez Pinson (1460-1523), who had won great confidence during the first travel of Christopher Columbus, sailed to coasts of the New World as soon as got patent of the king of Spain and approached the territory located at 8^0 south latitude – in the south of St. Augustine Cape of South America on January 20, 1500. Then he immediately changed the course towards the north-west and sailed towards today's Guiana. Pinson discovered outfall of the Amazon River during that travel (as seamen, who were at 200 km away from the shore, understood that, water of the river is fresh, they called it "Fresh Water Sea").

Diego Lepe: Another Spanish traveler by name Diego Lepe approached unknown land located at 10^0 south latitude on February 16, 1500 and noted that mentioned land extends towards the south-west. It means that, first of all Brazilian coasts were visited by Vicente Pinson and Diego Lepe, but not Pedro Cabral, so the discovery was made by them.

The king of Portugal had spies in ports of Spain and even in the palace of the kingdom, he received information by means of those spies when the Spain discovered new lands. They immediately gave information to Manuel I as soon as the travel of Pinson ended. So the king decided to hurry up.

The bull of the Pope Alexander VI had become trouble for Portuguese and Spaniards. Spaniards knew in which side of the demarcation line Big Anthill islands and Small Anthill islands of the Caribbean Sea were situated, but wandered through which part of unexplored lands located in the south of the Caribbean Sea that line passed before Cabral's expedition. So it became possible to carry out exploration below the 28th parallel.

After Vasco da Gama discovered eastern seaway to India and returned to the motherland, Spanish monarchs annulled monopoly of Columbus in West Hind and issue patent for sending expedition to those territories.

Pedro Alonso Nino: One of persons, who got one of first patents, was navigator Pedro Alonso (Peralonso) Nino who had participated at three travels towards the New World coasts and he sailed to the Caribbean Sea with one vessel at the beginning of June, 1499. Nino who respected Tordesillas treaty, organized expedition towards the part of north coasts of South America located in the west. First of all, he wanted to define distance between newly discovered lands and demarcation line.

Alonso de Okheda: Alonso de Okheda, who was participant of the second travel of Columbus towards coasts of the New World, got permission for exploring those coasts before Nino and sailed directly towards the continent located in the south of the Caribbean Sea with three vessels. As two vessels had been given him by Florentine bankers, Amerigo Vespucci also participated in the expedition.

Besides it, Chuan La Cosa, who had participated in the second expedition of Columbus and other well-known persons had been invited to the expedition. Okheda, who had prepared for the travel perfectly, analyzed the map of the Gulf of Pariah and Pearl Coast sent by Christopher Columbus to Spanish monarchs in 1498 before starting the travel. It proves that, he had sailed to coasts of the New World with the special mission. Following fact also proves it: some days after the expedition left the port of Cadis on May 18, 1499 he stopped one caravel on the way and made part of its staff to continue the expedition with him.

Amerigo Vespucci: Four vessels approached the coast in Oyapock Bay located at 5^0 or 6^0 south latitude and 51^0 west longitude at the end of June and were divided into two parts. Okheda continued his way towards the west-north-west with two vessels, but Vespucci sailed with the rest of vessels towards the south-west and saw outfalls of two large rivers flowing into the Atlantic Ocean – Amazon in the west and Para in the south on July 2 before Vicente Pinson. They filled barrels with fresh water at 45 km away from the coast. Amerigo Vespucci sailed 100 km towards inwards together with 20 companions in boats, saw that there were dense wood and returned to vessels after two days. Though they continued their way towards the east-south-east on Jule 24, couldn't overcome more than 250 km because of the current moving from opposite direc-tion. Thus, Spaniards discovered Guiana current which's speed was 3 km/hour and which was the branch of the South Passat.

Several scientists note that, Vespucci sailed 1200 km up to Turiasu Bay located at 1^0 $30^/$ south latitudes and 45^0 west longitude or to San Marcos Bay located at 2^0 south latitude and 44^0 west longitude and returned towards the north-west. Vespucci met Okheda near

Codera Cape after resting for a while in the island of Trinidad and they came to Spain in June of 1500.

Vicente Janez Pinson, who had participated at the first travel of Columbus towards coasts of the New World, left the port of Palos with four vessels bought with money of his relatives on December 1, 1499 and sailed directly towards Brazilian coasts. He changed the course towards the south-west in Green Cape Islands, passed the equator first of all his fellow-countrymen and unexpectedly approached San Roka Cape of Brazil (5^0 $30'$ south latitude) on January 26, 1500 after two-day ocean passage. Vicente Pinson went ashore together with notary and drove several wooden crosses into the ground. He declared that territory property of Spain kingdom in front of all staff.

After this discovery, Pinson continued his way towards the north-west and the coast disappeared from view after several days. Seamen, who saw that water of the ocean was fresh, began to sail towards the coast. Pinson reached the coast after overcoming 200 km and became the second person, who discovered outfall of Para River after Amerigo Vespucci.

Besides it, he discovered outfall of the largest river of the world after Amerigo Vespucci and called it Mar

Dulce ("Fresh Water Sea") (waters of the ocean were fresh near the continent). Then Pinson sailed towards the north-west and reached coasts of today's Guiana after Okheda. He explored 3000 km north coast line on his way and discovered 1200 km coast of the new continent. Experienced seaman understood that such coast line might only be specific for continent. But he thought that it was Asia. Thus, Pinson lost two vessels on the way and came to Palos with remained two vessels on September 29, 1500.

Bartolome Roldan: Diego Lepe left the port of Palos with two vessels in the middle of December 1499 two weeks after Pinson started his travel towards coasts of the New World. He sailed towards the south-west together with experienced navigator Bartolome Roldan and approached Brazilian coasts at 5^0 and $30^/$ south latitude on February 12. They continued their way towards the south and reached the most outlying point of South America – Saint Augustine Cape (Kabu Branku Cape, 7^0 south latitude). After sailing 200 km towards the south, they saw that coast extended to the south-west. Just after it Spaniards returned back and repeated Pinson's route. They entered Amazon, went up for about 400 km and Roldan noted all these facts in his new map.

Alonso Velez de Mendoza: They returned to Spain at the end of July of 1500, but after a while Roldan was invited to the next expedition to coasts of South America. The leader of that expedition was Alonso Velez de Mendoza - owner of the knight order and bankrupt nobleman. He left Seville with two vessels – *"San Cristobal"* and *"Saint Ghost"* (the second vessel was organized by brothers Luis and Anton Gerra) at the end of August and approached the coast at 30-35 km north of Kabu Branku Cape in November. Roldan showed himself as a real seaman and professional navigator during that expedition.

They continued their way towards the south without wasting any time and saw that the coast line extended to the south-west. Roldan reached outfall of the "Deer" River, may be San Francisco River on December 25 and rested there for several days. Vessels continued their way towards the south-west and reached the only large bay located in the north-east of the continent (Todos Santos, Bahia) and Jecitinonia River (16^0 south latitude) at the beginning of January of 1501. Alonso de Mendoza decided to return back just after it.

Though Spaniards couldn't find valuable stones at that territory, they explored about 1000 km coast line and noted it on prepared map. Both vessels returned to Seville at the end of May and at the beginning of June in 1501.

As Spaniards explored territories of Portuguese, results of Alonso de Mendoza's expedition had to be kept secret. They hoped to annul several paragraphs of Tordesillas treaty. Only after five centuries it became clear that, Bartolome Roldan approached Brazilian coasts before Cabral and could outline that territory.

The chronology proves that, expeditions sent by Spaniards to Brazilian coasts were organized systematically and the main task was to determine where that coast line extended to. So most of those expeditions were kept secret and their routes were coded.

First, Spaniards have discovered Brazil

Spaniards had other purposes in sending those expeditions to Brazilian coasts. They wanted to know exactly if there was land area on the demarcation line officially determined by Portuguese. After secret expeditions were sent to that territory, it became clear that, there were enough lands there and Spaniards understood that Portuguese had swindled them. But as the scale of deception wasn't definite, Spaniards couldn't protest against it. It needed to explore mentioned territory and so secret and permitted expeditions began to be sent there.

They were interested in one thing only: area of the land got by Portuguese in accordance with Tordesillas treaty and the latitude where it located. The border was definite owing to the meridian division and Spaniards wanted to know where that border extended to.

Pedro Alonso Nino explored those territories on the west of the demarcation line. Vicente Pinson went ashore and started exploration works at 8^0 south latitude, Diego Lepe at 10^0 30/ south latitude, Bartolome Roldan at 5^0 30/ south latitude, Alonso de Mendoza at 7^0 south latitude. Vicente Pinson, Diego Lepe, Pedro Alonso Nino and Alonso Okheda explored Brazilian coasts on the north-west after they went ashore, but Alonso de Mendoza did it on the south-west.

Amerigo Vespucci, who had participated in the expedition of Vicente Pinson, approached Brazilian coasts at 5^0-6^0 south latitude and sailed towards the south. He had to determine where southern coasts of Brazil extended to. But he couldn't fulfill his mission too. As if, all travelers had to prevent Spaniards' indifference in those territories in accordance with the special task.

Spanish monarchs wanted to know which part of lands located on the other side of the Atlantic Ocean became Portuguese's property after Tordesillas treaty. After the distance between parallels was calculated, it became clear that, they owned very large territory. It means that, Portuguese sea travelers owned very large territory without any trouble. May be, Portuguese, who pretended as simpleton when Tordesillas treaty was concluded, swindled Spaniards? They could increase the demarcation line for 270 liq during the second division and take the territory as large as today's Brazil from Spaniards.

Brazil belonged to Portuguese in accordance with Tordesillas treaty, but it had to be registered officially. After the discovery was registered, expeditions would be sent for exploration of that territory. Several candidates were presented to the king for realization of this work, but he chose Gonzalo Coelho. It is very interesting that, though that expedition was very important, name of its leader was kept secret for several centuries. The great adventurer Amerigo Vespucci showed this travel as his own achieve-ment. As if, he was the leader of that expedition in 1501-1502. But justice is restored sooner or later.

Gonzalo Coelho, who had left coasts of Portugal in 1501, was known as the assistant of Vespucci for a long time. It had been mentioned in several sources that, Vespucci had explored northern coasts of South America within the expedition of Alonso Okheda. He visited coasts of this continent during the expedition of Coelho for the first time. Vespucci was non-official navigator within the expedition of Coelho sailing to Brazilian Coasts and he had to write everything happened during the exploration. His notes are still remaining together with several maps of *"Santa Cruz"* or *"Land of parrots"* – coast line of Brazil together with rivers and bays made in XVI century.

Thus, captain-general Coelho left Lisbon with three vessels on May 10, 1501 and met with the expedition of Cabral returning from Green Cape Islands on June 1. His mission also was considered partly secret. But in spite of it, he had got some information about Cabral's travel to Brazilian coasts and understood that, travelling to the west of the Atlantic Ocean was easier than travelling to India and south of Africa.

They met with Fernando de Noronha Island surrounded by rocky places after five-week ocean passage as soon as found fresh water in Bijagos archipelago during 11 days and reached the coast of the continent on August 17. Portuguese stayed in the first cape for a week and then continued their way. Two seamen went ashore in order to establish commercial relations with indigenous population, but didn't return back. Though Amerigo Vespucci offered to punish Hindus, Coelho sailed towards the south without any conflict. As exploration of the coast line was especially significant, every point was noted exactly. Every point was called by names of holy persons. Those names show which point they visited first of all in the north.

Some scientists write that, a number of seamen used to make efforts in order to discover Brazil. A man by name John Jay organized an expedition on his own account in order to discover the Brazil Island in 1480. He thought that, it was situated in the west of Ireland. After six-week travel, the expedition returned back without achieving any results.

Seamen reached Angra dos Reis bay on January 6, San Vicente Island (24^0 south latitude) after 16 days and outfall of Cananea River at the end of January (25^0 south latitude and 48^0 west latitude). There Coelho completed his works and decided to return to the motherland. One of vessels of Ferdinand de Noronha left the marine and came to Lisbon on June 24, 1502.

We met with the fantasy of Vespucci when chronology of this expedition is analyzed. According to his information, remained two vessels left Brazilian coasts on February 13, continued the expedition towards the south, overcame 3000 km and met with new land at 52^0 south latitude on April 3. I. P. Magidovich and V. I. Magidovich suppose that this land was Trindade Island located at 20^0 south latitude and 30^0 west longitude. There seamen asked the captain-general to return back and they reached coasts of Sierra-Leone on May 10. There Gonzalo Coelho burned one unfit vessel, continued his way and dropped anchor in Lisbon on September 6, 1502.[1]

---

[1] И. П. Магидович, В. И. Магидович. Очерки по истории географических открытий, II том. Москва, "Просвещение". 1982. стр. 59

Though the expedition couldn't find any gold and silver, it could achieve great geographical successes. It explored 3000 km coast line between San Roka Cape and Cananea River from 5^0 $30^/$ south latitudes to 25^0 south latitude, 1000 km from 5^0 $30^/$ south latitudes to 16^0 south latitude and included them in the new map.

Achievements of that expedition kept as secret for 450 years and Vespucci had significant role in it. He hadn't mentioned name of Coelho when wrote about the expedition and misappropriated all achievements of the mission. Only at the end of 60th years of XX century, an old map of 1504-1505 was found in the library working in Fano, Italy. Brazil was called **"Land of Gonzalo Coelho"** in that map. After it, it became clear that, Gonzalo Coelho had played significant role in exploration of Brazil.

It is necessary to analyze geographical points where Coelho approached in order to determine real purposes of Portuguese, to learn if Cabral reached Brazil by accident and if any traveler visited that continent before Pedro Cabral.

The expedition approached San Roka Cape at 5^0 $30^/$ south latitude in the north on August 17. That cape had been discovered by Pinson and Lepe a year before.

Portuguese had to work there in order to disconsider exploration works carried out by Spaniards in that territory as the territory might be lost later. Portuguese had to prove that vessels of Pinson and Lepe approached Brazilian coasts in the east of the demarcation line and results of their activities had to be disconsidered. Portuguese had to end Spaniards' activity in accordance with juridical documents.

Several sources prove that, Coelho didn't know at which latitude Cabral approached Brazilian coasts. But it doesn't seem convincing as Cabral sent Gaspar de Lemos to Lisbon on May 1 in order to inform the king about the "discovery" after Brazilian coasts were seen. So we may note that, Gaspar de Lemos met Coelho in Lisbon and got information about Brazil. Thus, Coelho knew that, Cabral had approached the coast at $16^0 30^/$ south latitude (today's Porto Seguro).

Coelho, who could disconsider Spaniards' achievements sailed towards the south and reached Saint Augustine (Kabu Branku) Cape on August 28. He met with well-man-nered Hindus in the south and three Hindu women agreed to go to Portugal together with comers. Seamen stayed there for a month and then passed outfalls of small rivers flowing from Borborema mountains – San

Miguel (September 29), San Geronimo (September 30) and San Francisco located at 10^0 $30^/$ south latitude (October 4). The expedition approached Todos Santos bay located at 13^0 south latitude on November 1. It was the coast of the largest bay of the territory and later it began to be called "Bahia" (Bay). In Porto Seguro the expedition took two sea boys left by Cabral a year and a half before. It proves that Hindus were peaceloving people. Portuguese, who continued their way, left the outfall of Santa Lucia (Dosi River) behind on December 13, passed San Tome Cape (22^0 south latitude) on December 21, again sailed towards the west and reached amazing Guanabara Bay on January 1. They thought that it was the outfall of the river (23^0 south latitude) and called it Rio de Janeiro – "January River".

Though members of the expedition sailed to Brazilian coasts in order to explore those places in accordance with the official statement, they had more important task in reality. According to that task, Coelho had to determine at what distance of the eastern or western part of the demarcation line fixed in accordance with Tordesillas treaty the territory "discovered" by Cabral was situated. As if, previous expedition hadn't been able to determine coordi-nates of the coast. Portuguese did it in order to disguise the lie described in Tordesillas.

Thus, three caravels of Coelho went down for 500 km from the point they had approached in the coast and reached the outfall of large river on the first day of 1502 (territory of today's Rio de Janeiro).

Vespucci sailed to those coasts during the second expedition (1503-1504) together with Coelho, described most events happened during that travel in his writings and published them in Europe for several times. I want to note that, the mentioned travel could end with tragedy.

Good offices of Martin Behaim and explanation of questions concerning Brazil

But Portuguese ignored everybody, who had discovered Brazil, especially Pinson and Lepe and noted that the Portuguese seaman Duarte Pacheco Pereira and German scientist Martin Behaim working for Portugal had visited those territories in 1490-1495, but it was kept secret in order to prevent visit of other people. Though arguments were enough, it hadn't been proved yet.

Several scientists note that, German geographer Martin Behaim (1459-1507) sailed South American coasts within one of secret expeditions. This thought is considered frivolous as Behaim was weak scientist and unprofessional navigator. Portuguese exploring coasts of Africa – skilful seamen, captains, boatswains and navigators were masters of the navigation school established by Enrique in Sagrish. In accordance with several sources, Martin Behaim settled in Azores in the middle of 90th years of XV century and it is still unknown what he was occupied with there. In several scientists' mind, German scientist travelled western coasts of the Atlantic Ocean within secret expeditions of Portuguese and may be approached South and North American coasts.

Historians explain it as following: if Behaim sailed in the Western Atlantic, he could reach coasts of both continents. In accordance with several hypothesizes, he knew territories between Floridian peninsula and Brazil before 1498. Behaim had discovered South America with anonymous captains of Portuguese's vessels and had given necessary information to Cabral for the discovery of Brazil.[1]

If Martin Behaim had reached South American coasts and islands located around it, he had to note those territories on the biggest globe made by him in Nurnberg in 1492. Besides it, he could write special notes about mentioned lands after travels ended. He could also make maps describing outlines of coasts of the New World, which was interesting for seamen as an air and water. Behaim knew that, maps of unknown and newly discovered lands were the most valuable documents of that time.

The scientist's map didn't include any detail about the southern continent located on the other side of the Atlantic.[1] Thus, as there isn't any historical document, it hasn't been proved that, Behaim reached America in 90th years of XV century.

Some scientists note that, even old seamen's maps made in 1440 when the prince Enrique (Henrique) lived, prove that, one of Portuguese's vessels approached today's Pernambuco state of Brazil. Unfortunately, this

---

[1] Хенинг Р. Неведомые земли. Пер. с нем. М., 1963, т. IV, гл. 198.
[1] Дитмар А. Б. От Птолемея до Колумба. М. 1989, С. 230.

sensational fact couldn't be affirmed as there weren't enough documents. The reason is as following: Information about sea expeditions organized in Lisbon was coded at that time as powerful sea countries of Europe – kingdoms as Venetia and Aragon organized expeditions in order to discover unknown territories located on coasts of the Atlantic Ocean and competed with Portugal in this field.

Andrea Bianco had made a map of large territory and had written an illegible legend. In Julia Oldham's (1894) mind, Portuguese had discovered Brazil in 1448. When he read the legend, came to the conclusion that, "one of islands was situated at 1500 miles towards the west". Oldham thought that, it was Brazil, which was situated at 1520 miles towards the west of Green Cape Islands. The Portuguese scientist Batalia Reich supported Oldham's opinions concerning this problem, but this idea didn't spread through the community.[1]

It is considered frivolous hypothesis as Portuguese sea travelers could misappropriate discovered lands if they reached Brazilian coasts. It was reasonless to keep this

[1] Дж. Бейкер. История географических открытий и исследований. Перевод с англ. под редакцией и с предисловием Магидовича И. П. М., «Издательство иностранной литературы». 1950. стр. 44.

fact secret. Portugal didn't afraid of neighbor countries as Castilia was busy with Reconquista, Venetia struggled with Genoa and Arabian pirates in order to be hegemon in the Mediterranean, Ottoman Empire fought with Byzantine, and 100-year war continued between France and England. It means that, Portuguese sea travelers hadn't reached Brazil or coasts near it. But it doesn't mean that, they hadn't organized expeditions in the Atlantic Ocean.

Portuguese travelers carrying out research in the Atlantic Ocean

Portuguese discovered all islands near north-western coasts of Africa and Pyrenean peninsula during 45 years and included them on the territory of the Portugal kingdom. Vessels of two Portuguese noblemen, who had sailed to the Cape Bohador in 1419 – Juan Gonsalvich Zarku and Tristan Vash Tashera moved away from the west at the result of the storm, met with the island covered with dense wood and created basis for the discovery of Madeira Island. The expedition sent from Portugal towards the west under the leadership of Gonzalo Velu Cabral according to the task given by the son of the king of Portugal Juan I – Prince Enrique (1394-1460) discovered Azores in 1427-1432. Alvise (Luici) Cadamosto from Venetia and Antonio Usodimare from Genoa discovered Cabo Verde (Green Cape) islands in 1456.

In general, Portuguese sea travelers – Jal Ionsh (1435), Afonso Gonsalves Baldaia (1436), Anthony Gonsalves, Nunu Tristan (1441), Lanzarote Pisania (1444-1445), Dinesh Dias (1445), Alvaro Fernandez (1446), Arish Tinoku (1447), Diego Gomes (1456), Alvise Cadamosto, Antonio Usodimare (1456), Antonio Noli from Genoa (1460), Diego Afonso (1462), Pedro de Sintra (1461-1462), Fernan Gomez (1469), Sueiru da Costa (1470), Juan de Santaren, Pedro de Iskular (1471), Rui Siqueira (1472), Fernando Po (1472), Diego Azanbuj (1481), Diego Can (1482-1484 and 1485-1487) and Bartolommeo Dias (1487-1488) began to discover all western coast of Africa and to prepare for future sea travels.

Thus, Portuguese settled in Madeira in 1425, in Azores in 1432, and occupied Green Cape Islands in 1460. Diego Gomez came to Lisbon from Gambia in

1456 and brought 180-pound gold sand. That gold had been given him by indigenous population in exchange for simple glass decorations. Though this news spread in Castilia in the shortest time, he couldn't carry out his activity in the Atlantic Ocean because of the Reconquista. Portugal used this opportunity and increased influence in the Atlantic Ocean.

Expeditions of Portuguese sea travelers Jal Ionsh, Afonso Gonsalves Baldaia, Anthony Gonsalves, Nunu Tristan, Lanzarote Pisania, Dinesh Dias, Alvaro Fernandez, and Arish Tinoku had explored only north-western coasts of Africa and didn't move away from the coast of the continent before 1448.

There was great need for scientific theories of scientists, navigators, geographers, cartographers, astronomers and mathematicians in the discovery of unknown lands in the ocean. That's why every work of scientists was interesting for sea travelers and organizers of travels. Well-known scientist of Florence lived in XV century and worked in fields of astronomy, medicine, geography and mathematics Paolo dal Pozzo Toscanelli (1397-1482) had great authority in kingdoms of Apennine peninsula and in whole Europe.

Translation of **"Geography"** written by Greek scientist Claudius Ptolemy lived in II century into Latin made him popular and famous world map made in 1474 brought him fame in Europe. Paolo Toscanelli told the king of Portugal Alfonse V that, the earth was round and it was possible to go to India through the west: "I'm sure that, if the earth is round, existence of this way may be affirmed. In spite of it, I send the map I had made in order to simplify your work.

Route in the west, islands, coasts and the place you have to travel have been described on that map. The distance you have to keep from the equator and pole has also been fixed. Though it is known that, the place where spices finish and precious stones are found is east, I described that place in the west. You can reach that place if you go through land..." The scientist, who didn't afraid of wrath of the Catholic Church, defended his ideas in accordance with scientific theories and especially the work by name **"Almagest"** of Ptolemy (he noted in that work that the earth was spherical). Several scientists noted that, it was possible to meet with several continents on the western way to India.

It is necessary to pay special attention to this problem. What did the king Alfonse V think about ideas of the scientist? It is known that, such serious projects and ideas were discussed in **"Mathematical Union"** consisting of scientists, mathematicians, astronomers, cosmographers and geographers and their importance was determined.

The project of Columbus, which was presented to the king of Portugal Juan II after several years, was also discussed in **"Mathematical Union"** and the decision was negative. So he wasn't provided with vessels for organization of an expedition towards the western part of the Atlantic Ocean.

After ten years – in 1484 Columbus presented another analogous project to the king of Portugal Juan II. The idea of the Genoese seaman thinking that it was possible to travel to India through the west was simple. The earth is round and the largest part of it is land – Europe, Africa and Asia. So the distance between the western coast of Europe and eastern coast of Asia is small: it is possible to reach India, Chine and Japan in the shortest time by passing the Atlantic Ocean through the west. Such thought corresponded to ideas of geographers of that time.

Besides Paolo Toscanelli, Aristotle, Pliny the Elder, Strabo and Plutarch also thought that, such travel might be realized. The idea of Common Ocean was accepted by the church as well. Such theory was affirmed by the Islamic world including well-known Muslim geographers – Masudi, Al-Biruni and Idrisi.

Portugal decided to sign contract with the kingdom of Spain in order to avoid conflict with the powerful neighbor. If the official contract signed with participation of the Pope didn't exist, Spain could impede activity of expeditions of Portugal working in the Atlantic Ocean and pretend to discovered land. They signed contract with Madrid in Alcasovas in 1479. According to that contract, South America came under surveillance of Portuguese and Spaniards kept being hegemon in Canaries. According to the Pope's bull **"Aeterni Regis"**, kings of Spain Ferdinand and Isabella refused all known and unknown lands located in the west of Canaries for Portugal on 21st of June, 1481. It means that, vessels of Spain couldn't go down from the 28th parallel of the northern hemisphere.

Meeting of Alonso Sánchez de Huelva with Christopher Columbus on Madeira Islands

Theoretically, half of Floridian peninsula, Anthills, Mexico and South America became properties of Portugal. After **"Aeterni Regis"** came into force, historians began to note that, America had been discovered by Portuguese seamen before 1481 and this fact had been kept secret till the convenient time. This thought was defended by all annalists of XVI century – Bartolome de las Casas, Francisco Lopez de Gomara and Gonzalo Fernandez de Oviedo y Valdes, even Peruvian annalist Garcilaso de la Vega (son of the Ink prince and the hidalgo of Estremadura) mentioned name of Alonso Sanchez de Huelva as the seaman, who discovered the continent. Besides it, Jorje Blon, Francisco de Gomara Alonso and others noted that Huelva had met Christopher Columbus.

According to historical sources, Columbus travelled to Portugal for the next time in 1478 and settled in Madeira Islands for several years. The Genoese seaman got acquainted with his future wife Felipa de Perestrella there and married her in 1479. This marriage was windfall for Columbus. Owners of home where he had entered had been participants of expeditions organized by Enrique and other kings. Father of Felipa was from Lombardy and died twenty years ago. He had become nobleman of Enrique for his services in sea travels of Portugal and had been appointed governor of Porto Santo Island (Felipa's brother became governor of that island after Columbus's death).

According to information given by the merchant and sea traveler of Venice Alvise Cadamosto, father-in-law of Columbus was well-known colonialist. Christopher Columbus could find several documents about different travels of Portuguese in the Atlantic Ocean. Those documents helped him in preparation of the project about the discovery of the western part of the mentioned ocean.

Christopher Columbus started to learn practical navigation in Porto Santo and after travelling to Azores enlarged knowledge in expeditions to Guinea realized in 1482 and 1483. According to sources, Columbus was appointed commander of two vessels in accordance with representation sent by his brother-in-law to the king of Portugal when sailed towards Guinea and he could reach San Jorge da Mina port built by Diego Azanbuj on coasts of Guinea.

In 1484 Alonso Sanchez de Huelva, who was from the settlement of Niebla (Huelva), used to carry some goods from Spain to Canaries with his vessel. He carried fruits from Canaries to Madeira, then brought sugar and jam from Madeira to Spain. Ones Alonso Sanchez met with heavy hurricane when sailed from Canaries to Madeira. He sailed for about 28 or 29 days under the influence of that hurricane and approached an unknown island in the ocean. It is supposed that, that island was today's Santo Domingo. People came to that conclusion as the hurricane (east wind) blew in the direction from Canaries to Solano.[1]

Ones a wrecked vessel approached the coast of Porto Santo. Columbus noticed one weakened navigator among survived seamen. One of seamen raved about songs of motley birds, unknown animals and colored people. The vessel had been sailing from the west and struck the coast. Christopher Columbus took half-dead navigator home.

He looked after his guest and it became clear that, navigator's name was Alonso Sanchez de Huelva. After

---

[1] Горсиласо де ла Вега. Текст воспроизведен по изданию, История государства Инков. Л. «Наука». 1974. стр. 16-17.

getting better, Alonso Sanchez explained everything that happened to them. It became clear that, they had lost their way in the dark sea (then Atlantic Ocean was called like that) and reached very charming island. Sanchez informed his liberator about the place where the island was situated.[1] After it he died as other survived seamen of the wrecked vessel.[2]

According to Peruvian annalist Garcilaso de la Vega, historian Francisco Lopez de Gomara had written about the adventure of Alonso Sanchez de Huelva in his work **"General history of India"**. Son of the Ink prince caviled at that work as following: "De Gomara heard this information from ordinary persons – seamen and civil people, his father and father's authoritative friends, including people, who were close to the palace".

This adventure was told by the bishop Joseph Acosta for the first time. When he was in Peru, he heard that, one seaman had discovered coasts of the New World at the result of heavy hurricane and showed the way to Columbus as the Genoese seaman helped him after the catastrophe happened on the way to Madeira. Columbus

---

[1] Жорж Блон, «Атлантический океан», стр. 15.

[2] Франциско-де-Гомара. «Общая история Индий», 1552 г., XIII глава, «Первая открытия Индии».

told this story to some acquaintances including courtiers, and they helped him in organization of the expedition.[3]

Alonso Sanchez de Huelva didn't play any role in discovery of the New World

Spanish monarchs had to keep promises if Columbus could discover coasts of the New World. Obstacles began to be put in the way of the Genoese seaman, who had demanded great concessions. Columbus could get those concessions partly. People, who were close to the palace, prepared intrigues against the seaman who had become admiral after the first travel.

Conquistadors noted that, America had been discovered by Alonso Sanchez (de Huelva – R.D.). It was said because there was an inheritance conflict between heirs of Columbus and leadership of Castilia at that time (1510-1550). That's why courtiers tried to prove that,

---

[3] Горсиласо де ла Вега. Текст воспроизведен по изданию, История государства Инков. Л. «Наука». 1974. стр. 17-18.

lands located on the other side of the ocean hadn't been discovered by Columbus.[1]

Historians, who were against Columbus, noted that, II Juan wanted to entrust Sanchez with discovering those lands as he was in the west after surviving in the catastrophe. Columbus rendered the navigator harmless as he had prepared his own project for the discovery of places located in the west of the Atlantic Ocean and didn't want any competitor in this work.

This thought is so preconceived because when seamen of the wrecked vessel approached the coast, there were a lot of people besides Columbus and explanations were made with participation of them. Peruvian annalist Garcilaso de la Vega, Francisco Lopez de Gomara and Jorje Blon didn't want to deny services of Columbus when mentioned name of Huelva and noted that he had met the famous traveler. They only wanted to emphasize that, the Genoese seaman had got necessary information for realization of his transatlantic travel from Huelva. But as Columbus was very experienced navigator, he couldn't believe in such unserious, inexact information. He was sure that, America was far from Madeira Islands and it was

---

[1] Путешествие Христофора Колумба. М., 1956. Свет Я. Колумб. 1973.

impossible to reach there without knowing coordinates. Alonso de Huelva might meet with any island – even with Green Cape Islands.

This strange thought can't cast a shadow on the authority of Christopher Columbus. It was written in Garcilaso de la Vega's book that, Alonso Sanchez sailed in an unknown direction for 28-29 days under the influence of the hurricane and approached Santo Domingo Island. How it was possible? It means that, the vessel, which was pushed towards the west, met with Gulfstream current and could run away from it easily. It isn't convincing as in that case Portuguese could discover unknown lands located in the west of the Atlantic Ocean before the first travel of Columbus. Portuguese had sent there expeditions under the leadership of Vogado, Telles and Van Olmen, but none of those expeditions resulted in success.

Gulfstream current, which played the role of barrier in front of Big Anthill islands and Small Anthill islands, could take any vessel to Europe in the east of the Atlantic Ocean. It means that, the captain using North Passat blowing from east to west in the northern hemisphere wasn't able to take his vessel to the Caribbean aquatory as the North Passat rises towards the north and unites with Gulfstream at that latitude of the Atlantic Ocean.

If information of Huelva had positive influence on the project of Columbus, the Genoese seaman could follow the North Passat current during his first travel as soon as he left European coasts, directly reach South American coasts and discover Brazil. As Christopher Columbus had sailed near coasts of Guinea before, he was aware of existence of that current.

Development of shipbuilding, navigation and geography resulted in achievement of great successes in the field of great geographical discoveries. There was need for experienced and skilful seamen for realization of long-distance travels. Columbus owned all those characteristics. He (Columbus - R.D.) had got systematical education and learned geography, cartography and navigation as the person, who was interested in everything… He had married with the daughter of the Portuguese seaman in Porto Santo Island, so could get sea maps and diaries of his father-in-law.[5]

Christopher Columbus had prepared for the transatlantic travel seriously unlike most candidates and could realize it successfully. He didn't need Alonso de

[5] История средних веков. Абрамсон М. Л., Кириллова А. А., Колесницкий Н. Ф. и другие. Под редакцией Колесницкого Н. Ф. – 2-е издан. исп. и доп. – М., «Просвещение». 1986.стр. 393.

Huelva's help. He had begun to work on his project before 1484 and didn't want to change it. I had given detailed information about it in my work **"The scientist passed ahead of centuries – Nasiraddin Tusi".**

If we consider real discovery of Brazil and base on incorrect official information, we can surely note that, initial discovery of that territory was also made by Spaniards. But French historians note that, the vessel of their fellow-countryman Jan Cousin approached Brazilian coasts by accident at the result of storm in 1488. It is difficult to believe it, as vessels of the French didn't approach the equator and north-western coasts of Africa because were afraid of Portuguese and Spaniards. But French historians write that, Jan Cuzen's travel was registered in the navigation archive of Dieppe port in France.

Scientists, who note that, Brazil had been discovered before Pedro Cabral, are divided into two groups. Most of them note that, Portuguese sailed to Brazilian coasts several years before the first travel of Columbus, but some of them emphasize that, officials of Lisbon knew that territory after 1492. I investigated activity of Christopher Columbus carried out in Lisbon first of all in order to elucidate this problem.

The succession of events proves that, Columbus informed Portuguese about the opportunity of sailing to Brazil after he returned from the first travel. Owing to him, the king Juan II decided to send there secret expedition.

Some islands on the Atlantic Ocean were known by Muslim scientists

Christopher Columbus presented his transatlantic project to the king Juan II at the beginning of 1484 when lived in Por-tugal. But that time wasn't convenient for the monarch of Portugal. Then the king was busy with suppressing revolt raised in the country by magnates. Besides it, he was interested in expeditions towards western coasts of Africa.

It is known that, Columbus had asked the king to give him many privileges for his services after the expedition completed successfully. To ask such privileges was insolence. Nobody, even well-known noblemen hadn't asked such privileges before Columbus. What were demands of the Genoese seaman? He had demanded to be admiral of the Atlantic Ocean, title of nobleman, to be vise-king of lands, which had to be discovered, one tenth of incomes of those lands, eight percent of money, which would be earned at the result of the trade, which would be carried out in new lands and gold spurs. Juan II, who kept his noblemen under the strict surveillance, couldn't give mentioned privileges to anybody.

If Juan II was very strict and harsh monarch, why he didn't reject Columbus directly? First of all, seaman's project had to be analyzed by scientists. The project was presented to **"Mathematical Union"** of Lisbon where the most talented and skilful scientists and mathematicians of Portugal worked under the leadership of the archbishop of Ceuta Diego Ortiz de Villegas. Some of members of that organization were Jewish scientists. Rodrigo, who had improved astrolabe and sextant, and expert of the navigation astronomy Hose Vitsingo were among those scientists. Mentioned persons thought that, measures and distances hadn't been fixed correctly in the project. Though those scientists also didn't know exact sizes of the Earth, they were sure that, calculations of Columbus were wrong.

It is not known which decision was made by that council, but it is known that, decision made in 1485 wasn't in favour of Columbus. The Genoese seaman's wife died in the same year and he decided to go to Spain.

As soon as the Genoese seaman left Lisbon, the king Juan II decided to send an expedition to the west of the Atlantic Ocean in order to check his project. The king and his advisers made this decision by common consent.

At that time the **"Island of Seven Cities"**, Haldat and Anthelia Islands located in the west of the Atlantic Ocean were discussed in the Pyrenean peninsula and most countries of Europe. Portuguese sea travelers had organized several expeditions for the discovery of those islands.

Scientists of the middle ages and ancient times were interested in Haldat islands or Islands of Good Luck very much. Some scientists, especially remarkable Azerbaijani scientist, founder of Maraga observatory Muhammad Nasiraddin Tusi (1201-1274) noted that, those islands were situated at 35^0 km towards the west from Greenwich meridian.

English scientist G. R. Kaye, who was interested in this problem very much, noted in his work **"Astronomy**

of India" that, Islands of Good Luck were situated at 35^0 towards the west from Greenwich meridian.[1]

Why did G. R. Kaye think so? Most of scientists of the middle ages and ancient times thought that, Islands of Good Luck were in the west of the Atlantic Ocean.

Remarkable scientist of the Mamun Academy establishhed in Khorezm Abu Raihan Al-Biruni (973-1048) wrote about it as following: "Some scientists calculate the initial length from Islands of Good Luck, but some of them start calculation from the coast of the West Sea. Difference between these two places is 10^0".

Arabian geographer of Spain Ali ibn al Magribi al Andaluzi, Syrian scientist, employee of Maraga observatory Gregory Abul Faraj, remarkable scientist of that observatory Gutbaddin Shirazi, well-known geographer and historian of XIII century Mahmud el-Caswini and well-known Arabian scientist of XIV century Harrary had different scientific ideas about those islands.

Harrary's explanation is more interesting: "Western lands start from the West Sea. Nobody had seen another side of this sea and nobody knows what there are. Most

---

[1] Г.Р. Кае «Индийская астрономия» 1924, стр. 52

of islands have been settled. Two of them are called Algeria Haldat. They are the largest islands".

This thought of the Arabian scientist surprised the Professor Habibulla Mammadbayli, who had investigated scientific heritage of Nasiraddin Tusi, and he wrote following thoughts: "Harrary's notes are very interesting, he had written about western lands and Anthelia Islands. The Atlantic Ocean was called West Sea in the middle ages. Islands mentioned by Harrary might be Canary Islands, Azores, Green Cape Islands or Anthelia Islands. As Canary Islands, Azores and Green Cape Islands don't consist of many islands and there aren't great differences between them, they couldn't be considered by Hararry. It seems that, Harrary mentioned Anthelia Islands in his writing.

Two of Anthelia islands – Cuba and Haiti are larger than others...

Then these two islands are Algeria Haldat, which was mentioned by Harrary..."[1]

If Harrary had written about Anthelia Islands at the beginning of XIV century, there had to be some

[1] H.C.Məmmədbəyli, Mühəmməd Nəsirəddin Tusi. Bakı, "Gənclik", 1980. səh. 160-161.

information about those islands in geographical literature, especially on maps published after it.

Ancient scientists noted that Anthelia Islands were situated in the east of Asia. Really, maps describing mentioned islands had spread widely in Europe.

Italian cartographer Francesco Pizziano had made a map describing Anthelia Islands in 1367. That map is kept in the library of Parma at present. Besides it, another map made by the unknown cartographer in 1424 is kept in Weimar, Germany. That map had been made by the German scientist Humboldt. The French cartographer Battista Beccaria had made a map in 1435. Besides the name of Anthelia, its synonym Stanahia also had been written on that map. In 1436, the Italian cartographer Andrea Bianchini had made the Big Venetian map, which described Anthelia Islands. The Italian scientist Paolo Toscanelli described Anthelia on the centre of the Atlantic Ocean on his map made in 1474.

Researches of new lands on the western of Atlantics

Most of mentioned maps were discussed by European scientists. Scientists knew that, coasts of the Atlantic Ocean located in the west of the Old World weren't endless and there wasn't any doubt that, there was large land area in the west. But distance between that territory and European coasts was unknown.

All these facts had to be checked. The king Juan II entrusted the Frenchman by name Ferdinand van Olmen known in Portugal as Fernando de Ulmo with realization of this work, he didn't choose Columbus for this purpose.

Ferdinand van Olmen's fellow-countrymen had worked as governor in one of Azores. He also was governor of one island before the travel. At that time, most seamen, financers and merchants serving Portugal used to organize expeditions with their own capitals, for example, Cortereal brothers had organized such expeditions in 1500, 1502 and 1506. S. Morison, Ch. Verlaine, Vadim Magidovich and Iosif Magidovich noted in their works: "Van Olmen united with a colonialist by name Estreito from Madeira when he organized his expedition. According to words of van Olmen, he wanted to discover several islands located in the west of the Atlantic Ocean or coast of the continent. He called the country he had to discover the **"Island of Seven Cities"** as didn't know its name".

Of course, this thought is confusing. Van Olmen had gone to expedition in accordance with the king's order and he had to check Columbus's project practically.

Ruling committees of Portugal didn't pay enough attention to unknown western part of the Atlantic Ocean before Paolo Toscanelli's well-known map was made. Everybody wandered if there were unknown islands in the west of Canaries, Madeira Islands, Azores and Green Cape Islands. Portuguese organized travels towards the west of mentioned islands in the middle of XV century. In 1462, the king Alfonso V gave great privileges to the person by name Vogado for appropriating about two islands located in the west. The seaman by name Telles searched for Anthelia and the **"Island of Seven Cities"**. Many seamen travelled after him, but nobody achieved any success.

At that time following rumour had spread in Portugal: Islands, which can't be discovered, are seen from a distance. Of course, it is impossible to believe in such unserious thought. If islands were seen in the ocean, then the king Alfonso V could send there at least one expedition in order to explore those islands. There wasn't any doubt that, there were islands in the western part of the Atlantic Ocean (near mentioned islands). Columbus also agreed with this thought. But he believed that, there were mythic Anthelia and other islands on the middle of the ocean. The Genoese seaman thought like that because of the letter of Toscanelli. It was possible to use those islands as stopping-places in the ocean passage on the way to Asia.

Van Olmen knew results of travels of Vogado and Telles and knew that, it was impossible to use any island as the stopping-place on his way to India through the west, so his expedition would meet with great difficulties. That's why though Juan II gave permission for organization of the expedition he had doubts about its success. Otherwise he could organize the expedition with his own capital.

The king would give many privileges to van Olmen in 1486 if the expedition completed successfully as he had organized the travel on his own account.

"Mathematical Union" told the king that, Columbus had prepared his project owing to Paolo Toscanelli's calculations. That's why Olmen had to explore the Atlantic Ocean in accordance with those calculations. May be, the project of the Genoese seaman had been copied when it was in **"Mathematical Union"** and that copy had been given to van Olmen.

Van Olmen started his travel with two caravels in spring of 1487. He planned to pass the Atlantic Ocean in 40 days. I want to mention that, in 1492, Columbus had overcome the distance between Canaries and Bahamas in 36 days. When the Professor Charles Verlinden read the declaration of the French seaman, he noted with surprise that, Portuguese seamen had sent secret expeditions to the west of the Atlantic Ocean before 1486, they knew which islands were on the other side of the ocean and where the unknown continent was situated.[1]

I don't agree with this thought of Ch. Verlinden. If van Olmen knew the place where unknown islands and large land area were situated, he could easily discover those territories. Besides it, if Portuguese seamen knew the east coast line of the New World, Portuguese could choose the meridian, through which the demarcation line had to pass, when the Pope divided the Earth between two kingdoms in accordance his bull in 1493. But it didn't happen. As it is known, Portuguese achieved their

---

[1] Чарльз Верлинден, Покорители Америки: Христофор Колумб. "Феникс", Ростов-на-Дону. 1997 г., стр.23.

goals only when Tordesillas was concluded in 1494. If above mentioned assumptions were true, representatives of Juan II might demand to move the demarcation line for 470 liq towards Anthill Mountains discovered by Columbus, but not for 370 liq towards the west from Green Cape Islands. Thus, Portuguese didn't know that, there was any other island or large land area in the Atlantic Ocean in the west of Canaries, Madeira Islands, Azores and Green Cape Islands.

Then how could van Olmen pass the ocean in 40 days? It is obvious that, he reason is different from above mentioned factors.

In Portugal Christopher Columbus said that, he will pass the Atlantic Ocean in about 30 days in order to reach the eastern coast of Asia. Van Olmen shared this thought with Juan II after he looked through the Genoese seaman's project. It means that, the French seaman's expedition travelled in accordance with the transatlantic project prepared by Columbus besides the map made by Paolo Toscanelli.

Columbus was considered real candidate, who would conquer the Atlantic

Christopher Columbus, who was an experienced and skilful seaman of his time, didn't expect such events. That's why he had presented the project consisting of incorrect digits. He had another map, which he didn't show anybody, even to his native relatives (would be called *"Lost map of Columbus"* in future). That's why van Olmen couldn't achieve any success during his travel.

The French sea traveler, who had seriously prepared for the mentioned travel, planned to return to coasts of Portugal after six months. But he couldn't achieve any success. The reason of the failure of van Olmen and Estreito may be as following: they started their travel in inconvenient period of the year and didn't use Passats properly. Bartolome de las Casas – one of annalists, who had described in his writings occupation of New World coasts by conquistadors, – wrote about the travel of Ernan de Olmos (Probably he considered Ferdinand van Olmen) in one of his stories. He wrote: "That travel took him to the western coasts of Ireland, to the north of the route determined by Columbus".

Unfortunately, van Olmen couldn't return from that travel. Ch. Verlinden wrote: "In spite of all these, the French seaman, who worked for Portugal, might discover America before the Genoese seaman, who worked for Castilia. Then, history of the west would be different. If Olmen could achieve his goal, language of Brazil and other 17 countries of Latin America might be Portuguese.[1]

Sometimes fortune of the history depends on the fortune of one person!" If Juan II accepted Columbus's offer, language of former colonies located in the western part of the Atlantic Ocean might be Portuguese.

After analyzing both expeditions, I can decisively note that, Columbus had prepared for the travel more seriously than the French seaman and could achieve his goal owing to his efforts. Members of the **"Mathematical Union"** couldn't forgive themselves for their mistake after Columbus's expedition achieved success.

---

[1] Чарльз Верлинден, Покорители Америки: Христофор Колумб. "Феникс", Ростов-на-Дону. 1997г., стр.24.

Christopher Columbus, who had prepared very well and was an experienced seaman, left the port of Palos on August 3, 1492 with 90 persons and three vessels – *"Santa Maria"*, *"Pinta"* and *"Ninia"* according to the consent of Spanish monarchs Ferdinand and Isabella. He discovered today's Watling island of Bahamas on October 12 and called it "San Salvador".

Unlike Spaniards, Portuguese didn't believe that, Columbus had reached the East Asia. Some scientists couldn't believe that, outline of the Earth is so short when analyzed the admiral's route. But there were skeptics in Spain, who worked alone.

I think that, Christopher Columbus couldn't agree with thoughts of the Florentine cosmographer. First of all, well-known sea traveler couldn't agree with length of the Earth's outline. It means that, Asia isn't situated in the Atlantic Ocean at 10000-12000 km away from Canaries in the west as Paolo Toscanelli thought. Columbus had determined that, land area located in the west of the Atlantic Ocean is at 4500-5000 km away from Europe. It means that, the mentioned land was other land, which was unknown for the Old World. This idea of the sea traveler wasn't fortuitous. I explained it in my work **"The scientist passed ahead of centuries – Nasiraddin Tusi"** in detail.

An Italian humanist Pietro Martire (Poignant Peter), who lived in Barcelona and were close to the kingdom palace, corresponded with his fellow-countrymen. He had written in the letter written on November 1, 1493: "One person by name Colon (Columbus) says that, he could reach India, the place of antipodes of the west. He discovered many islands located on the other side of the East Ocean near India as cosmographers thought… I don't want to write anything about it, nevertheless size of the Earth made me to think otherwise".

That is, before the travel, Christopher Columbus thought otherwise about calculations of Paolo Toscanelli as Pietro Martire. Doubtless, Christopher Columbus, who had read a lot of scientific literatures, might think as Pietro Martire.

Duarte Pacheco Pereira and unofficial discovery of Brazil

Some historians note in accordance with the treaty concluded in Alcasovas that, Portuguese sea travelers had discovered lands located below the 28th parallel and in the western part of the Atlantic Ocean before 1479, but hadn't registered it officially. It means that, those lands became property of Portugal in accordance with the bull of the Pope Sixtus IV. At the result of it, wars with Castilia were ended.

Though improvement of vessels simplified management at those days, navigation was realized in accordance with the direction of the wind and movement of currents. It means that, it is possible to reach today's Brazilian coasts and to return back by means of winds and currents.

Some scientists write that, a number of seamen used to make efforts in order to discover Brazil. A man by name John Jay organized an expedition on his own account in order to discover the Brazil Island in 1480. He thought that, it was situated in the west of Ireland. After six-week travel, the expedition returned back without achieving any results.

Merchants of Bristol had been sending 2-4 vessels each year in order to discover the Brazil Island since 1490, but couldn't achieve anything.[1]

As English seamen sailed in northern latitudes only, they couldn't discover today's Brazil. Besides it, they didn't want to enter territories of Spaniards and Portuguese.

According to historical sources, participant of Cabral's expedition – Duarte Pereira had been in lands located on the other side of the Atlantic Ocean. It may be seen unconvincing.

As Cabral had to register the "discovery of Brazil" when travelled to India, he needed a person knowing those coasts very well in order to prevent any unexpected events on their way. This person was Pereira.

Well-known captain, explorer and cartographer Duarte Pacheco Pereira (1469-1533) had participated in expeditions in western coasts of Africa after II part of 80th years of XV century, met an accident near the Principle Island in 1488 and was rescued together with several seamen by the expedition of Bartolommeo Dias, who was returning from the Cape of Good Hope. He had participated in several secret expeditions, which's route, geographical coordinates and coast lines were coded.

[1] Дж. Бейкер. История географических открытий и исследований. Перевод с англ. под редакцией и с предисловием Магидовича И. П. Москва, «Издательство иностранной литературы». 1950. стр. 44.

Duarte Pereira spent several years of his life for sailing in the eastern and middle part of the Atlantic Ocean and exploring unknown islands located in those areas. There wasn't any thought about large territory yet. As only three continents were known at that time, ordinary seamen couldn't think that, there might be fourth and fifth continents in the ocean. Thus, seamen of XV century didn't know that, the Earth was larger than they know. But Pereira could reach Brazilian coasts in accordance with the secret task. The date of that history is unknown.

Pereira noted in his work **"Esmeraldo de Sita Orbis" ("Emerald about the position of the Earth")** written in 1505-1508 that, he had visited lands located on the other side of the Atlantic Ocean. As that work was a copy, scientists didn't know what to think. Only three volumes and part of the fourth volume of the work consisting of five volumes (books) were found in Portugal libraries, those volumes were published and presented to the community in 1892 for the first time.

The author gave information about existence of lands located on the other side of the Atlantic Ocean in the mentioned book and noted that he had visited those lands six years before Cabral's expedition.[1]

Some scientists wanted to use this fact and to show Pereira as the discoverer of South America in 1494. The discovery of South America by Pereira was described in the large article of I volume of Pereira da Silva's work **"The history of the Portuguese colonization of Brazil"**. J. Rocha Pombo noted that the Portuguese sea traveler had reached America before Cabral and Columbus. If we analyze Pereira's activity, we can elucidate a number of questions.

Though original documents don't exist, it is convincing that, Pereira had approached Brazilian coasts before Cabral. Concrete date is also mentioned as 1494. I also determined at the result of my investigations that, Pereira could reach Brazilian coasts first of all. Sometimes we need to use simple ways in order to solve complicated problems. What is this simple way?

I will elucidate obscurities of the treaty of Alcasovas by investigating this question. It is known that, according to some scientists, Portuguese were aware of existence of Brazil before 1480 and that's why could ask the Pope for opportune articles.

---

[1] И. П. Магидович, В. И. Магидович. Очерки по истории географических открытий, II том. Москва, "Просвещение". 1982. стр.55

First of all, I plan to look through bulls of Popes about division of the world. After it, I understood that Portuguese visited Brazilian coasts at the beginning of 1494.

1000 km trajectory of the Canary current is the most perspective way for passing the Atlantic Ocean from east to west in the northern hemisphere. That's why though the ocean river flowing from north to south at 20^0 west longitude and through African coast line from 30^0 east latitude to 10^0 east latitude with the speed 10-30 sm/san was slow, it could assist vessels for approaching equator. An average depth of the Canary current is 500 meters. It is known that, Columbus used this current during his transatlantic travel. Van Olmen, who wanted to realize his project, also tried to use mentioned current. But one of them succeeded, when other failed. Why did it happen? A little mistake made during the ocean passage resulted in tragedy.

Columbus, who tried to learn characteristics of currents started from western coasts of the Atlantic Ocean, had determined that currents couldn't move on the straight line. The mentioned river turns to the left and to the right. When the Genoese seaman entered the current's embrace, he decided to sail towards the west. But van Olmen sailed to the western part of the ocean by means of Canary and North Passat currents and left those coasts by means of the Gulfstream. He had to wander away from that route when vessels sailed towards the north.

Pereira also could meet with such tragedy. But it was winter when he fulfilled the king's task. I'll explain this problem in the next part according to the chronology.

Discovery of the New World had ended hegemony of Portugal

Portuguese appropriated north-western coasts of Africa when Castilia was busy with the war for freedom against Arabians. As Portuguese wanted to legalize it, they asked Nicolas V, who had owned throne of Saint Peter in Vatican, to sign a decree. The bull **"Dum diversas"** was signed on June 18, 1452 and it was the first historical document on division of the world. The Portugal king Juan I asked the Pope to explain the situation in order to prevent chaos. That's why the Pope Nicolas V noted in his bull **("Inter caetera")** signed on January 8, 1455 that, monopoly of the trade with African coasts belonged to Portuguese. In fact, Africa became property of the Portugal king.

But in spite of it, only 1479 may be considered "the year of change" for Portuguese. The Atlantic Ocean was divided into two parts in accordance with the treaty concluded in Alcasovas in September of the same year. Castilia's consent was necessary in this problem. The Pope Sixtus IV invited both parties to negotiations on June 21, 1481 in order to confirm the treaty of Alcasovas and acquainted them with the bull **"Aeterni Regis"**.

Though the Pope respected Isabella, he gave all territories located in the south of Canaries to Portugal. It became clear that, Portuguese had given presents to Roman Pontifical Councils. That's why Sixtus IV agreed with all demands of Portuguese. Besides it, the Portugal kingdom demanded territories of Castilia and didn't deviate from war. But Castilia didn't want to return any span of lands to its neighbor.

The king Alfonso V, who gave up his demands for territories of Castilia could get very convenient privileges for Portugal: Canaries remained as the property of Castilia, but Azores and Madeira Islands were registered as the inseparable territory of Portugal. Spanish vessels hadn't to go below the 28th parallel of the north hemisphere when organized any expedition. Half of the Floridian Peninsula, Anthill Islands, Mexico, Panama and South America became property of Portugal in theory.

The treaty of Alcasovas couldn't last for a long time. Spaniards demanded to divide the world again peacefully after the first travel of Columbus. It had become clear that, there were large territories in the west of lands discovered by Columbus. Spaniard Rodrigo Borgia born in Xativa located near Valencia became the owner of Saint Peter's throne in Vatican. Other interesting fact: the bishop of Aragon was appointed Roman pontificator when Columbus started his first transatlantic travel (August of 1492). He was the second person from Aragon, who was appointed for such high position. First person was bishop of Valencia Alonso de Borgia, who was the Pope with the name Callixtus III.

Nobody expected such coincidence. New Pope Alexander VI (Borja or Borgia) signed the bull **"Inter caetera"** on May 4, 1493. According to the bull, lands discovered by Spaniards in the western part of the Atlantic Ocean were given to catholic kings (Ferdinand from Aragon and Isabella from Castilia – R. D.).

Population of those lands had to be converted to Christianity. The demarcation line was moved for 100 liq away from Azores in order to prevent interference between two kingdoms. Now I want to write about unofficial discovery of Brazil again. I consider dates noted by historians groundless. Historians wrote that, Brazil was discovered in 1480 or 1490 (accurate date hasn't been written), names of Jan Cousin, Alonso Huelva, Martin Behaim and others have been linked with the discovery. The most convincing date is considered 1494. Why?

Christopher Columbus completed his first travel to coasts of the New World on March 15, 1493. It means that, Spaniards might reach lands located in the western part of the Atlantic Ocean unexpectedly. But there is incomprehensibility in this question: they mightn't demand territories located below the 28th parallel according to the treaty signed in 1481. Because territories located below 28^0 east latitude belonged to the Portugal throne according to the treaty signed in Alcasovas. In spite of it, Spaniards couldn't sail below the 28th parallel and tried to conceal it.

Every lost day was against Portuguese after coasts of the New World were discovered. Portuguese heard about this discovery first of all after Columbus returned to European coasts as admiral's vessel had approached Madeira Islands mechanically and had sailed to Lisbon after it. The king Juan II received Christopher Columbus in his palace after the discovery was made. The king decided to make decisive steps after that meeting. So Juan II organized secret expedition towards coasts of the New World.

Probably, Duarte Pereira was appointed leader of that expedition as mentioned above. Next processes and Pereira's work **"Esmeraldo de Sita Orbis" ("Emerald about the position of the Earth")** written in 1505-1508 showed that he had sailed to Brazilian coasts six years before Cabral.

Pope VI Alexandr Borgia divides the world into two parts

As it is known, the bull **"Inter caetera"** signed by the Pope Alexander VI less than two months after the discovery of the New World coasts – on May 4, 1493 at the urgent request of Spanish monarchs surprised Portuguese. According to this document, all territories located at 100 liq west of Azores became property of Spaniards at the result of Columbus's travel. Agreeing with such division minimized activity of Portuguese in the Atlantic Ocean. Following question occurred: if there isn't any large territory having strategic importance and significant geographical location in the west of the mentioned demarcation line and below 28^0 east latitude, what is the significance of the endless ocean? Then people thought that, there wasn't any land area in the west of Azores, Madeira Islands and Green Cape Islands.

Expeditions of Vogado and van Olmen couldn't achieve any success in mentioned parts of the ocean.

Spaniards had achieved their goal in accordance with the bull of Alexander VI on May 4. Now it was Portuguese's turn. If Columbus could leave Canaries and discover large land area in the west, Portuguese could do it too. As seafaring and navigation had developed highly in Portugal, Portuguese also could leave one of islands located near the Pyrenean peninsula and discover unknown lands in the west. Southern part of Africa had already been conquered and way out to the Indian Ocean had been opened.

One question worried everybody: what was the distance between those lands and the Old World and at which latitudes were they situated? King Juan II knew very well that, Columbus's travel had lasted for seven months. But it was unknown, how many days he had sailed in the ocean. In spite of it, the king didn't want to waste time in vain. Secret expedition began to be prepared by Portuguese.

Thus, real discovery of Brazil may be made clear. The expedition had to be started in 1493. Probably, preparation works were realized out of the Pyrenean peninsula and in Madeira Islands. As hot days had passed and stormy weathers were characteristic for autumn of those latitudes, this work had to be carried out on the north-western coast of Africa. They had to use other islands in order to prevent risks. From this standpoint, the most convenient geographical location was the location of Green Cape Islands and remote western point of Africa located near the Gulf of Guinea.

Portugal, which didn't want to declare its regard for the mentioned division, began to declare dissatisfaction after a year and demanded the Pope to move the demarcation line for 270 liq towards the west. Representatives of both kingdoms met with the participation of Alexander VI in Tordesillas in 1494 and the demarcation line was moved for 370 liq away from Azores (for 2200 km towards the west from those islands) according to the next treaty concluded on June 7. According to the treaty of Tordesillas, all territories located in the east of the demarcation line belonged to Portugal, but lands located in the west belonged to Spain.

In a word, Spain was considered owner of America except Brazil and Portugal was considered owner of Africa and India according to the Pope's bull.[1]

Portuguese were lucky as Columbus was on coasts of the New World when they held negotiations with Spaniards in Tordesillas and they could realize their purposes. If the Genoese seaman was in Spain, he

---

[1] История средних веков. Абрамсон М. Л., Кириллова А. А., Колесницкий Н. Ф. и другие. Под редакцией Колесницкого Н. Ф. – 2-е изд. исп. и доп. – М., «Просвещение», 1986. стр. 393.

wouldn't allow to move the demarcation line for 270 liq towards the west as he knew that, there was a land area on the west of the prime meridian found by Tusi (the line located at 34^0 towards the west from today's Greenwich meridian) and Portuguese wanted to appropriate that territory by moving the demarcation line for 270 liq towards the west.

It was too late when Columbus returned from his travel – Portuguese could deceive Spaniards and signed Tordesillas treaty.

Authority of Spain increased in Europe as soon as the Reconquista ended in that kingdom (1492). Arabian emirates of the Pyrenean Peninsula began to disappear from the political map since the beginning of VIII century. The Pope Alexander VI, who took into consideration all these facts, began to treat Spanish kings respectfully. Historians think that, the mentioned pontificator had played exceptional role in appropriation of the continent located in the western part of the Atlantic Ocean by Spain. Because he had declared Spain owner of those territories in his bull **"Inter caetera"** signed on May 3, 1493 after Columbus completed his first travel. Besides it, Alexander VI entrusted Castilia and Aragon.

with management of the church in the Pyrenean Peninsula and newly discovered lands

In March, as soon as Columbus returned from his first travel, Spanish monarchs asked the ambassador Bernardino de Karvahala (relative of Hernan Cortes and bishop of Badajoz), who was in Rome, to activate his activity there. The ambassador did his best and made the Pope to sign well-known bull **"Inter caetera"** in two months. Adoption of that bull demanded great responsibility from Alexander VI as he didn't want to interfere in works of his ancestors and to trample on rights of catholic kings. Because Spaniards had discovered unknown lands on the other side of the Atlantic Ocean and they had to convert population of those territories to Christianity in accordance with well-known bull.

It was noted in the document that, islands and large land area located in the west towards India, in the place where vessels didn't pass should be given to Spanish kings. The pontificator, who didn't want to irritate Portuguese, mentioned that, Portuguese would have authorities in Africa, Guinea and Gold Coast (the coast line located in the north of the Gulf of Guinea) and

Spaniards would have same authorities in lands located on the other side of the ocean.

The Portugal king Juan II didn't want to declare his dissatisfaction at first, but after several months he began to defend de facto rights concerning those lands taking into consideration the treaty signed in 1481. After it, the Pope was obliged to look through his decision again, invited parties to negotiations after a year, on May 4 and made concessions to Portuguese. A month after that date, on June 7, Alexander VI made some changes on the treaty signed a year ago in Tordesillas, made some concessions and ratified that document. The treaty of Tordesillas may be considered a victory of Portuguese as the demarcation line was moved for 100 liq towards the west from Azores in accordance with Spaniards' offer in 1493 and for 370 liq towards the west from Azores in accordance with Portuguese's insistence.

Special commission of Portuguese and Spaniards had to determine location of the demarcation line before the end of 1495 in accordance with the treaty of Tordesillas. But this task couldn't be fulfilled because of the discontent between Spaniards and Portuguese cosmographers (The conflict occurred between two kingdoms in 1512 for lands located in South America as it was expected).[1]

All territories located in the left of 38^0 west longitude were given to the jurisdiction of Spanish monarchs according to the treaty concluded on May 4, 1493. Portuguese began to think about adequate steps as soon as heard it.

Portuguese diplomatists made urgent steps before the treaty of Tordesillas. They understood that, the territory located on the other side of the ocean will be lost and that's why tried to organize direct negotiations with Spaniards. Christopher Columbus began his second travel towards coasts of the New World with 17 vessels and 1500 persons on September 25, 1493, when the representative of Portuguese was on his way to Tordesillas. Before this event, in July Alexander Borgia published the third copy of his bull signed on May 3 with the name **"Eximiae devotionis"**. This document offered compromise for both parties.

Before parties solved the problem without interference of the Pope, Alexander VI issued his fourth bull in December, 1493 with the name **"Dudum siquidem"** and

---

[1] Португальская колониальная империя, СИЭ, т. 11, с. 451-452.

showed its date as September 25. After that document was issued, Portuguese protested against the Pope as all territories between the demarcation line and eastern part of India had become property of Spain. Nevertheless, India was the territory of Portugal in accordance with the treaty of Alcasovas and Spaniards had agreed with that document. Portuguese noted that, the present treaty was against their interests. They hadn't any way for sailing to India as Bartolommeo Dias (1488) had discovered remote western point of Africa before the travel of Christopher Columbus and had found way out to the Indian Ocean.

The fourth bull of the Pope Alexander VI issued in December of 1493 brought Portuguese to bay and they decided to make urgent steps. They decided to send expedition to coasts of South America. Then Portuguese knew that, Columbus had travelled to lands he had discovered for the second time.

Reserve route of Portuguese to Brazilian coasts

Real seaman and professional navigator must learn something at the result of previous travels. If Pereira would use Canary and North Passat currents, he could repeat van Olmen's mistake. But it was winter in the northern hemisphere when he started his travel. It was better to use alternative currents in order to avoid hurricanes and to try not to meet with vessels sailing under the flag of Spain.

The most convenient current for sailing towards the west in the middle of the ocean was West Passat. Because the mentioned current starts in coasts of the Gulf of Guinea between 1^0 north latitude and 2^0-3^0 south latitude (width of the current is 300-350 km there) and its width increases when extends towards the west. Broadening ocean river covers the territory between 2^0 north latitude and 5^0 south latitude in the Cape Palmas. Width of the current became 8^0-9^0 (800-900 km) at 10^0 west longitude. The current have, a branch moving towards the north-west in the west of the Ferro Island and its width extends to the coast of 20^0 or 30^0 east latitude. The South Passat has two branches near the San Roka Cape on Brazilian coasts – Guiana current moving towards the north to the Caribbean basin and Brazilian current extending towards the south to South Winds.

The speed of this current moving from Africa to South American coasts isn't constant: it is 4-5 km in a day at the beginning, 8-12 km on the meridian of the Cape Palmas (in summer), 6 km at 10^0 west longitude, but sometimes it may be 11 km a day.

Probably, Duarte Pereira entered the South Passat current near the entry of Guinean coasts and sailed towards Brazilian coasts. He couldn't impede the ocean river, which took the expedition to the considered point. Pereira drew outlines of that coast line as a cartographer and determined coordinates of that place. He returned back without wasting time. Hastiness didn't let him complete his work.

To my mind, one of main tasks of the secret expedition sent by the king Juan II to the western part of the ocean was to return to the motherland as soon as needed lands are discovered. This task was fulfilled. Members of the expedition might lose a month if they tried to get water and to repair the vessel. That's why old mistake was repeated after six years during the travel of Pedro Cabral.

What was that mistake? As exploration of discovered lands demanded waste of time, it didn't correspond to the king's task. Portuguese seamen had to leave mentioned coasts as soon as the land was discovered. That's why Pereira thought that, he had discovered an island besides a continent as he hadn't time to check the coast line. Columbus also declared that, he had discovered a group of islands after his first travel. Cabral also thought that, the territory discovered by him was a large island when he saw it for the first time.

In spite of all these, Pereira returned to Lisbon in the first quarter of 1494. Every detail of the prepared report was checked seriously. All distances between Lisbon, remote western coast of Africa, Madeira and Green Cape Islands and Brazilian coasts were fixed in the report. Special attention was paid to coordinates of the discovered territory. I looked through some versions of coordinates and came to the following conclusion: Pereira had reached Brazilian coasts at 1^0 south latitude and 42^0-43^0 west longitude in the territory of San-Luis and Belen. As the coast line is cracked in that territory and the territory of San-Luis is situated on the peninsula, the seaman thought that, he had met with a group of islands.

You may ask why I emphasize that, Pereira reached the territory of today's San-Luis. I think that, Pereira sailed towards the west by means of the South Passat current near Guinean coasts and met with Guiana and Brazilian currents in the threshold of South America. As the Guinea current moving towards the north rose to latitudes of the Pyrenean peninsula, Duarte Pereira chose that current and sailed to 1^0 south latitude. It was easier to return to Europe from that latitude without wasting time.

Though Columbus's report of coordinates had been coded, Portuguese presumably knew that, Spaniards had met with lands at 50^0 west longitude. Pereira wasn't interested in latitudes before the beginning of 1494. Two factors played important role in this problem. First, Spaniards mightn't carry out exploration below the 28th parallel of the northern hemisphere according to the treaty of Alcasovas. Otherwise, made discoveries wouldn't have any juridical basis. Second, Pereira decided to use the South Passat moving towards the west below the equator as he had to fulfill the king's task in winter. Owing to it, Portuguese achieved their goals. But they couldn't even imagine that, the territory they had discovered was a continent.

The expedition organized in accordance with the order of the king Manuel I after six years, sailed from Green Cape Islands towards the south under the leadership of

Cabral. They sailed towards the west by means of the South Passat current and approached the coast line by means of the Brazilian current blowing towards the south Pereira's efforts are matchless in this business. But participation of experienced seamen might reveal secret of the expedition.

As Bartolommeo Dias knew the Atlantic Ocean, it was impossible to convince him of the lie about losing way in the ocean. But in spite of all these, though Bartolommeo Dias had understood the ruse, he took this secret to the bottom of the ocean.

The most experienced, the most skilful and well-known seamen of the Pyrenean peninsula Bartolommeo Dias and Duarte Pereira were members of Pedro Cabral's expedition. So they couldn't lose way in stormy weathers. Those persons knew the eastern part of the Atlantic Ocean very well and were graduates of the most authori-tative navigation school. Besides it, they were close friends as Bartolommeo Dias had rescued Pereira, who had met an accident when returned to Lisbon after the discovery of the Cape of Good Hope.

The difference between them was as following: Bartolommeo Dias knew western coasts of Africa located between north and south, but Pereira knew islands and archipelagos located in the Atlantic Ocean, which were known for Portuguese seamen. As he knew places of archipelagos and currents very well, he had to be entrusted with the discovery of Brazil. That expedition hadn't to fail as expeditions of Vogado, Telles, van Olmen and others.

But Cabral's expedition to India was the last travel for Bartolommeo Dias, who had discovered the Cape of Good Hope for Europeans. According to historical sources, the expedition met with strong hurricane at the end of May when it left Brazilian coasts and reached the Cape of Good Hope. At the result of it, four vessels of the expedition went down the ocean. Bartoıommeo Dias died on that tragic day.

One of persons, who knew secrets of Brazil's enigmatic discovery - annalist of the expedition Pero Vaz de Caminha also died during that travel. He was killed together with 50 members of the expedition when indigenous population attacked Portuguese in Calicut. Main witnesses took secrets of Brazil's discovery to the life hereafter. It corresponded to the Portugal king's interests.

In a word, the Portugal kingdom could appropriate very large territory owing to Duarte Pereira.

Nevertheless, if that expedition resulted in failure as previous travels, they had to be satisfied with islands discovered in the Atlantic Ocean.

Portuguese, who had enough necessary information, demanded to move the demarcation line towards 50^0 west longitude in order to ensure fair division as if they didn't know anything about existence of Brazil. At that time almost everybody was sure that the earth's surface was straight. Portuguese knew that, this factor had to be taken into consideration in order to swindle the Pope by basing on the treaty of Tordesillas. As the earth's surface was considered straight, all territories extended from the west of the demarcation line to the east had to be Portuguese's property.

The king Juan II, who was satisfied with results of Pereira's expedition, asked his diplomatists to organize new negotiations. They had already prepared answers of questions, which would be given by Spaniards' representtatives and pontificator.

Portuguese planned to move the demarcation line for 370 liq instead of 100 liq towards the west from Azores at the result of negotiations with Spaniards held with participation of the Pope. The line was situated on the right of lands discovered by Christopher Columbus and near Europe. Representatives of Spaniards were sure that, Portuguese, who weren't aware of existence of western lands, wanted to own some additional water basin in the ocean in order to ensure security of their vessels. Why did representatives of Spaniards agree with demands of their rivals without any resistance? They didn't object to compromising useless ocean waters to Portuguese in order to avoid superfluous conflict.

Representatives of Portuguese benefited by results of the discovery made during Pedro Cabral's first travel as islands discovered by the Genoese admiral were situated at 65^0-70^0 west longitude and the territory discovered by Duarte Pereira was situated at 42^0-43^0 west longitude. As 25^0-30^0-buffer zone appeared between made discoveries, Portuguese were sure that, Spaniards wouldn't object to moving the demarcation line for 45-47^0 towards the west longitude.

It should be especially mentioned that, Portuguese were successful in that business too. Bahamas, islands of Haiti and Cuba were first lands discovered by Columbus during the transatlantic passage and there weren't any land in the east of them. Thus, if there was any territory in the east of known islands, Portuguese had an opportunity to appropriate it. Admiral's report described only ocean waters in the east of the 65th and 70th meridians. Portuguese, who used Spaniards' mistake, sent secret expedition to South American coasts hurriedly, discovered large land area in the east of the considered meridian and kept it secret. Juan II had to invite Spaniards to negotiations and to register secretly discovered lands officially.

Though negotiations hadn't any significance for some time, they were restored afterwards and the treaty of Tordesillas was concluded on June 7, 1494. As it is known, the demarcation line was moved for 370 liq – 46^0 30$^/$ towards the west from Azores and Brazil became property of Portugal. America became property of Spanish kings besides the remote western part of today's Brazil. But in spite of it, it wasn't considered victory of Spaniards. Thus, political geography of coasts of the New World was founded and the Pope sealed it up.

Thus, Portuguese swindled Spaniards by means of the Pope Alexander Borgia VI and appropriated Brazil which's total area was equal to 8,5 milion square kilometers. That unjust division disclaimed efforts of Spaniards as Brazilian coasts were visited by Spanish sea travelers Vicente Pinson and Diego Lepe for the first time. Portuguese should be grateful to Duarte Pereira, but not Pedro Cabral for being owner of Latin America. Most seamen weren't successful in discovering lands in the west of the Atlantic Ocean though following task was given to them. But Pereira could achieve mentioned goal. The experienced captain discovered lands, which were very important for the king Juan II, and could return to Europe before next negotiations held with Spaniards. Besides it, he participated in negotiations held in Tordesillas and swindled Spaniards by means of the Pope. The captain was obliged to keep this secret till the day he died.

It should be mentioned that, Portuguese could swindle their rivals as able hypnotizers. They pretended as if Spaniards had appropriated their lands. At the result of it, the demarcation line was moved towards the west.

The pontificator granted Ferdinand and Isabella titles of "Catholic Kings" in the same year.

Activities of Duarte Pacheco Pereira and Christopher Columbus

The king Juan II was satisfied with the treaty concluded with Castilia as Portugal was aware of existence of Brazil and it could appropriate it. Portuguese didn't know territories located on the other side of Brazil, they thought that, Brazil was situated in a large island as Madeira Islands, Azores and Green Cape Islands.

Portuguese should be grateful to Pereira, but not Cabral. After his travel, the longitude of Brazilian coasts was determined and the Portugal kingdom could appropriate Brazil.

Besides it, Pereira became well-known as the military commander in the next years. He travelled to Cochin City of India in 1503 and resisted to the army of 60 thousand fighters with 8 thousand soldiers. They wanted to banish Portuguese from India, but failed.

Pereira was appointed commandant of the Elmina fort, which was situated on the "Gold Coast" of Africa. But after a while, he became victim of intrigues and was on trial. He was accused of the false accusation – theft and corruption and was arrested. Though the seaman was fully exonerated afterwards, he lost his position, wealth and authority. He died in poverty and misery.

Spaniards began to send different expeditions to coasts of the New World before the third travel of Christopher

Columbus. Expeditions were organized in order to explore territories of Anthill Islands and continents located in the north and south of them. It means that, lands located in the south of 28^0 north latitude were becoming property of Spaniards.

Spanish sea travelers, who didn't want to pay attention to previous bulls of Popes, began to sail below the 28th parallel in stages in accordance with permissions of monarchs and to appropriate territories located there.

The expedition left Brazilian coasts on May 2 with 11 vessels, reached south of Africa without any difficulties and entered the strong storm near coasts of the Indian Ocean, at some distant from the Cape of Good Hope. Four vessels met an accident and went down there. Bartolommeo Dias, whom the king Manuel I trusted, was lost in the ocean. It is interesting that, brother of Bartolommeo – Diego Dias separated from the expedition with his vessel, reached Madagascar Island and founded discovery of the largest island of Africa. But Pedro Cabral thought that, he died as others and continued his way without carrying out any search. The expedition reached the port of Malindi located in the south-west of Africa and sailed to Calicut (today's Kozhikode).

Pedro Cabral, who reached India with some losses in accordance with considered plan, could found a factory in Calicut. But influence and authority of Muslim merchants impeded free activity of Portuguese and armed conflict occurred between tens of Muslims. About fifteen Portuguese seamen and talented writer Pero Vaz de Caminha were killed during that conflict. The city was bombed according to Cabral's order and all vessels of Muslims were burned. Then alternative trade relation was founded in Cochin.[1]

Portuguese, who was returning back at the beginning of 1501, lost another vessel near Mozambique and after salutary operation they sailed towards Green Cape Islands with four vessels. Diego Dias, who left the Madagascar Island by accident, met members of expedition in those islands and returned to motherland together with them.

It should be especially noted that, one of vessels of the mentioned expedition had separated from the staff on south-eastern coasts of Africa after the expedition returned from India and reached Lisbon first of all. So,

[1] История средних веков. Абрамсон М. Л., Кириллова А. А., Колесницкий Н. Ф. и другие. Под редакцией Колесницкого Н. Ф. – 2-е изд. исп. и доп. – М., «Просвещение», 1986. стр. 394.

they were invited to the kingdom palace and gave all necessary information about the travel and happened tragic events.

Why did I emphasize this fact? Cabral hadn't justified hopes of the king. Though his expedition was larger than Vasco da Gama's expedition for numbers of vessels and persons, he couldn't achieve any satisfactory result. But, fortunately, Duarte Pereira survived and Brazil was discovered officially.

The expedition, which had lost six vessels, came to coasts of the Pyrenean peninsula after a year and a half. It returned to the motherland with five vessels full of valuable goods on September 6, 1501.

The king Manuel I, who didn't pay any attention to the value of brought goods, was dissatisfied with the expedition's result as the expedition hadn't achieved considered goal. In spite of it, incomes of the expedition were more than twice.

The land discovered by Cabral was called **"Terra Brasilis"** or **"Santa Cruz"** on maps made in Europe in XVI century. But people called him **"The land of parrots"** or **"The land of Brazil"**.

Cabral was debarred from the palace and Vasco da Gama was appointed commander of the next expedition organized in 1502, though Cabral was appointed second captain, he deviated from participation in that expedition.

Former commander, who had lost all his fame, went to Beira Baixa in 1509 and lived there till the end of his life. But Manuel I issued salary for Cabral in 1515 for the discovery of **"Vera Cruz".**

Former commander, who was isolated from people and lived quietly, died in 1526. The sea traveler, who had been in coasts of four continents of the world – Europe, South America, Africa and Asia during only one travel, was buried in the general churchyard of the gothic church "Igreja da Graca". Rare trees were found in his garden. Those trees began to be brought to Europe as raw material for production of red-violet paint and discovered land began to be called Brazil in accordance with its name (pau-brasil).

Fortune of Pedro Cabral, who had reached India

Ordinary tombstone found in XIX century proves that, personality of the author of "The great discovery" wasn't considered significant in XVI century. And the writing found on the tombstone of the seaman's wife Isabel Kashtru shows that, she was maid of the daughter of the Portugal king Juan II.

The Brazilian historian Francisco Adolfo Varnhagen identified Cabral's neglected grave in 1848. Brazil and Portugal celebrated his 500th birth anniversary in 1968. Monuments were put to him in Lisbon and Rio de Janeiro for his services in appropriation of Brazil.

All important discoveries made before XVI century are enigmatic. Christopher Columbus, who wanted to discover a large continent for his heirs, has been buried in the Cathedral temple of Seville, Pedro Alvaresh Cabral, who had kept the secret of the king Manuel I till the end of his life, has been buried in the churchyard "Igreja da Graca", Amerigo Vespucci and Duarte Pacheco have been buried in Lisbon's town churchyard as common citizens. What were purposes of Portuguese monarchs? Did they want to swindle Spaniards in order to prevent armed conflicts? They could partly achieve this goal. Portuguese could swindle Spaniards by means of priests – owners of Saint Peter's throne. They did it without letting anybody to understand the situation.

Of course, the best way was to use carelessness as a pretext. Pedro Cabral used this way in 1500 and made Brazil property of Portugal. Credulous Spaniards, who were in euphoria after Columbus's first travel, were obliged to believe the nonsense contrived at the end of XV century. They preferred territories located near the Caribbean Sea to Brazil.

Achieved results

1. When everything is analyzed in succession, it became clear that, there were many obscurities in Pedro Cabral's discovery. His expedition passed equator after Green Cape Islands, continued its way towards the west and approached Brazilian coasts at 17^0 south latitude on April 22. San Nicolas Island is situated at 24^0 west

longitude, but Corumba Cape of Brazil is situated at 39^0 west longitude. It means that, the squadron had moved away from its southern line for 15^0 towards the west. It is equal to 1600 km.

Corumba Cape "discovered" by Pedro Cabral by accident, is situated at 17^0 south latitude. It means that, the expedition moved away from the main route and sailed for 1600 km in wrong direction. But it is not convincing. Because it was impossible to lose way as the expedition had a compass. It means that, Portuguese hadn't lost their way, they changed the course purposely, went Brazilian coasts by the course fixed beforehand and made above mentioned "discovery".

Experienced commanders and captains as Bartolommeo Dias, Diego Dias and Duarte Pacheco Pereira participated in that expedition, noted the distance they had overcome on their diaries every day and controlled the course of vessels. So they had to understand that the expedition had dodged from the main course and warn Pedro Cabral. But it seems that, the leader of the expedition was satisfied with this deviation and he entrusted his assistants with the course at the ocean passage.

It should be noted that, it is possible to determine the geographical latitude continuously when the weather is enough good. How Portuguese could lose the way in that case? All these facts prove that, they had sailed by the course fixed beforehand and achieved their goals.

2. It is interesting that, Portuguese put big wooden cross on the coast instead of the stone emblem indicating that mentioned territory belonged to the Portugal Kingdom. What it was? It was next negligence or discovered lands weren't so significant? Nevertheless, every sea traveler had to approach such discovery seriously as Portuguese searched for lands on that part of the Atlantic Ocean for tens of years and couldn't achieve any success. Though Cabral achieved this "happiness", he was indifferent to his "discovery".

It is known that, ten days after the discovery of Brazil the leader of the expedition sent Gaspar de Lemos to Portugal with his vessel and the letter he had written. Information about the discovery was usually sent hastily when discovered geographical point had special importance. It means that, the discovery of Brazil had been planned beforehand and the world community had to be informed about it.

3. Spanish monarchs began to send different expeditions to coasts of South America and especially Brazil after the treaty of Tordesillas was concluded. Vicente Pinson went ashore and started exploration works at 8^0 south latitude, Diego Lepe at 10^0, 5^0 $30^/$ south latitude, Bartolome Roldan at 5^0 $30^/$ south latitude, Alonso de Mendoza at 7^0 south latitude. Vicente Pinson, Diego Lepe, Pedro Alonso Nino and Alonso Okheda explored Brazilian coasts on the north-west after they went ashore, but Alonso de Mendoza did it on the south-west. Even Pedro Alonso Nino explored those territories on the west of the demarcation line.

Amerigo Vespucci, who had participated in the expedition of Vicente Pinson, approached Brazilian coasts at 5^0-6^0 south latitude and sailed towards the south. He had to determine where southern coasts of Brazil extended to. But he couldn't fulfill his mission too. As if, all travelers had to prevent Spaniards' indifference in those territories in accordance with the special task.

Main purpose of Spaniards was to learn if there was land area on the demarcation line officially determined by Portuguese. After secret expeditions were sent to that territory, it became clear that, there were enough lands there and Spaniards understood that Portuguese had swindled them. But as the scale of deception wasn't definite, Spaniards couldn't protest against it.

They wanted to know total area and latitude of the territory appropriated by Portuguese in accordance with the treaty of Tordesillas. After the distance between parallels was calculated, it became clear that, they owned very large territory. It means that, Portuguese sea travelers owned very large territory without any trouble. They could increase the demarcation line for 270 liq during the second division and take the territory as large as today's Brazil from Spaniards. It proves that, Portuguese were aware of existence of Brazil before the treaty concluded in 1494.

4. It is known that, Columbus firstly presented his project to the **"Mathematical Union"** of Lisbon, but mathematiccians rejected the Genoese seaman. But unexpectedly, search of lands in the west of the Atlantic Ocean was commissioned to the Flemish seaman Ferdinand van Olmen. He had to travel in accordance with the commission of the king Juan II and to check Colum-bus's project. Van Olmen started his travel with two caravels in spring of 1487. He planned to reach the Atlantic Ocean within 40 days. I want to mention that,

Columbus had overcome the distance between Canaries and Bahamas within 36 days (the Genoese seaman noted that, he could reach any coast in 30 days). It proves that, Portuguese wanted to explore considered lands in accordance with Columbus's project without notifying him. But as enough preparations weren't made, they couldn't do it.

In 1462, the king Alfonse V sent the seaman by name Vogado in that direction as the head of the expedition for discovery of unknown islands located in the west of the Atlantic Ocean. Another seaman by name Thelles searched for Anthelia or the **"Island of Seven Cities"** in the west of the ocean. Many other seamen travelled after them, but none of them achieved any goal.

By taking into consideration all these facts, I came to the following conclusion: Portuguese were unaware of existence of Brazilian coasts before 1493. If they had travelled to coasts of South America, representatives of Juan II could demand to move demarcation line for 470 liq towards Anthill islands discovered by Columbus, instead of 370 liq towards the west from Green Cape Islands in the treaty signed in Tordesillas in 1494. So, Portuguese were unaware of existence of any island or large land area in the west of Canaries, Madeira Islands, Azores, and Green Cape Islands.

5. As Portuguese travelled in accordance with Paolo Toscanelli's reports, they failed. But Columbus didn't agree with length of the Earth Circle calculated by the scientist. The Genoese seaman didn't believe that, Asia is situated in the west, 10000-12000 km away from Canaries as P. Toscanelli considered. So, he carried out individual calculations and proved that the land area located in the west of the Atlantic Ocean is 4500-5000 km away from Europe. It means that, that land area was unknown for the Old World. But Portuguese, who explored west of the Atlantic Ocean by means of several expeditions, were sure that, there wasn't any land area in that part of the ocean.

6. Most scientists noted that, several seamen had travelled to coasts of America including Brazil before Christopher Columbus. Alonso Sanchez de Huelva, Jean Cousin, Martin Behaim and others spread information about existence of those lands after sailing in above mentioned coasts. They said that, Columbus had prepared his well-known transatlantic project after the meeting with Huelva and the map prepared by Paolo Toscanelli in 1474. But my consideration is different and

after longterm investigations I want to note that, he had prepared his project in accordance with the astronomic catalogue **"Zij-i-Ilkhani"** prepared by Nasiraddin Tusi. But what is the relation between Christopher Columbus and Brazilian coasts?

After his first travel, Portuguese organized secret expedition hurriedly and could determine location of Brazil during a short time before Pedro Cabral.

After his first travel, Portuguese organized secret expedition hurriedly and could determine location of Brazil during a short time before Pedro Cabral. Some historians note in accordance with the treaty concluded in Alcasovas that, Portuguese sea travelers had discovered lands located below the 28th parallel and in the western part of the Atlantic Ocean before 1479, but hadn't registered it officially. It means that, those lands became property of Portugal in accordance with the bull of the Pope Sixtus IV. If this consideration is true, the world community could learn name of that traveler after passed years and centuries.

7. According to historical sources, Duarte Pacheco Pereira had been in lands located on the other side of the Atlantic Ocean. It may be seen unconvincing. As Cabral had to register the *"discovery of Brazil"* when travelled

to India, he needed a person knowing those coasts very well in order to prevent any unexpected events on their way. This person was Pereira.

Pereira spent part of his life in search of unknown islands in the eastern and central parts of the Atlantic Ocean. To my mind, Pereira had reached Brazilian coasts according to the secret task. But the year has to be specified.

Pereira's work **"Esmeraldo de Sita Orbis"** (**"Emerald about the position of the Earth"**) written in 1505-1508 showed that he had sailed to lands located on the other side of the Atlantic Ocean six years before Cabral. Though there weren't any original documents, it's convincing that, Pereira had approached Brazilian coasts before Cabral.

8. When studying the papal bulls concerning division of the world, I found out that it was 1494 when the Portuguese reached the land of Brazil.

Christopher Columbus finished his first travel to the New World on 15 March 1493. It means that Spaniards could unexpectedly come ashore in the lands located in the Western Atlantic. The Portuguese were shocked at the bull **"Inter caetera"** issued by Pope Alexander VI at insistence of Spanish monarchs on 4 May 1493 orless than two months after the discovery of the New World. According to this document, in the result of the Columbus' travel all lands 100 leagues west of the Azores were granted de jure to Spain. Acceptance of such division would mean minimization of all activities for the Portuguese in the Atlantics.

King John II was not going to waste any time. Preparation for a secret expedition was launched without the knowledge of Spain. This expedition was to have started out by the end of 1493.

Portugal, which hadn't express its attitude to this division before, voiced a complaint in respect of it a year on and demanded 270 leagues westward demarcation of the Pope. Representatives of both states met at Tordesillas in 1494 with the participation of Alexander VI, and according to the Treaty signed on the 7th of June the demarcation line was relocated 370 leagues (2200 km) west of the Azores. According to the Tordesillas Treaty all lands east of the demarcation line were granted to Portugal, and the lands west of this line were granted to Spain.

The Tordesillas Treaty was a victory of the Portuguese rather than of the Spaniard, because the demarcation line between these two kingdoms fixed 100 leagues west of the Azores on the suggestion of Spain in 1493had been relocated 370 leagues west of the Azores on the insistence of Portugal.

The fourth bulla issued by Pope Alexander VI in December 1493 stalemated Portugal, and the Portuguese decided to take a flexible step. They launched an expedition to the coast of South America. Especially since they could freelytravel to the lands discovered by Christopher Columbus.

9. Since it was dangerous to travel in the Northern hemisphere in winter, it's most likely thatPereira laid a course downwards for the Brazilian coast in December 1493. Willingly or unwillingly he brought the expedition to the destination at the powerful and great river. Pereira, as a cartographer, contoured the coastal area and specified its latitude and longitude coordinates. Then he returned homewithout losing any time.

Since Pereira wasn't able to explore the coastal area, he supposed that this land was not a continent but an island. After the first travel Columbus also declared that, he had discovered a group of islands in the ocean.

Probably, Duarte Pereira returned to Lisbon in the first quarter of 1494. I looked through some versions of coordinates and came to the following conclusion:

Pereira had reached Brazilian coasts at 1^0 south latitude and 42^0-43^0 west longitude in the territory of San-Luis and Belen. As the territory of San-Luis is situated on the peninsula, the seaman thought that, he had met with a group of islands.

I think that, Pereira sailed towards the west by means of the South Passat current near Guinean coasts and met with Guiana and Brazilian currents in the threshold of South America. As the Guinea current moving towards the north rose to latitudes of the Pyrenean peninsula, Pereira chose that current and sailed to 1^0 south latitude. It was easier to return to Europe from that latitude without wasting time.

Owing to the discovery of Brazilian coasts, Portuguese achieved their goals. But they couldn't even imagine that, the territory they had discovered was a continent.

The expedition organized after six years, sailed from Green Cape Islands towards the south under the leadership of Pedro Cabral. It sailed towards the west by means of the South Passat current and approached the coast line by means of the Brazilian current blowing towards the south. Portuguese wanted to learn only one thing: the total area of the land located on the other side of Africa. But, in spite of it, they couldn't understand that, the coast line they had approached was a continent. As they hadn't explored that territory enough, couldn't determine this fact yet. But Spaniards had understood after discovery of the outfall of Amazon that, the territory located in the east of the demarcation line fixed in accordance with the treaty of Tordesillas was a continent. They thought that, the rich river as Amazon might pass only the continent.

In a word, the Portugal kingdom could appropriate very large territory owing to Duarte Pereira. Nevertheless, if that expedition resulted in failure as previous travels, they had to be satisfied with islands discovered in the Atlantic Ocean.

10. Portuguese, who had enough necessary information, demanded to move the demarcation line towards 50^0 west longitude in order to ensure fair division as if they didn't know anything about existence of Brazil in 1494.

The king Juan II, who was satisfied with results of Pereira's expedition, asked his diplomatists to organize new negotiations.

Portuguese planned to move the demarcation line for 370 liq instead of 100 liq towards the west from Azores at the result of negotiations with Spaniards held with participation of the Pope. The line was situated on the right of lands discovered by Columbus and near Europe. Representatives of Portuguese benefited by results of the discovery made during Cabral's first travel as islands discovered by the Genoese admiral were situated at 65^0-70^0 west longitude and the territory discovered by Pereira was situated at 42^0-43^0 west longitude. As 25^0-30^0-buffer zone appeared between made discoveries, Portuguese were sure that, Spaniards wouldn't object to moving the demarcation line for 50^0 towards the west longitude.

The treaty of Tordesillas was concluded on June 7, 1494. As it is known, the demarcation line was moved for 370 liq – 46^0 $30^/$ towards the west from Azores and Brazil became property of Portugal. America became property of Spanish kings besides the remote western part of today's Brazil. But in spite of it, it wasn't considered victory of Spaniards. Thus, political geography of coasts of the New World was founded and the Pope sealed it up.

Thus, Portuguese swindled Spaniards by means of the Pope Alexander Borgia VI and appropriated Brazil. That unjust division disclaimed efforts of Spaniards as Brazilian coasts were visited by Spanish sea travelers Vicente Pinson and Diego Lepe for the first time. But

Pereira could achieve mentioned goal. The experienced captain discovered lands, which were very important for the king Juan II, and could return to Europe before next negotiations held with Spaniards. Besides it, he participated in negotiations held in Tordesillas and swindled Spaniards by means of the Pope. The captain was obliged to keep this secret till the day he died.

Portuguese should be grateful to Pereira, but not Cabral. After his travel, the longitude of Brazilian coasts was determined and the Portugal kingdom could appropriate Brazil.

Review - 1

Though Ramiz Daniz didn't ask help of any scientist when he wrote scientific research works **"Christopher Columbus, Nasiraddin Tusi and discovery of America", "The scientist passed ahead of centuries - Nasiraddin Tusi"** and **"Expedition to India discovers**

Brazil", remarkable scientists - full and corresponding members of ANAS have declared their reviews and opinions about these works.

Mentioned works made scientists of geography, history and astronomy to astonish. R. Daniz has discovered new investigation objects, tried to prove that, Columbus had used the astronomic catalogue **"Zij-i Ilkhani"** prepared by Nasiraddin Tusi in Maraga observatory when he discovered America, noted many aspects about the discovery of Brazil and declared decisively that, the Portuguese sea traveler Duarte Pereira had discovered Brazil six years before Pedro Cabral.

Azerbaijan founds economical, cultural and political relations with other countries, integrates with the world and foreign countries are interested in science, education and culture of our country. That's why scientific research works of Ramiz Daniz may be interesting for scientists and ordinary readers, who learn the history of geographical discoveries. Probably he'll be invited to scientific conferences held abroad. Because Ramiz Daniz has found out many novelties and could deny most stereotypes.

Scientists of the world will learn that, the history of geographical discoveries is investigated in Azerbaijan too and they'll wait for next works of Ramiz Daniz.

The scientific and practical conference devoted to 800th birth anniversary of the genius Azerbaijan scientist Nasiraddin Tusi was held by the name *"Scientific services of Nasiraddin Tusi and N. Tusi in the activity of the writer and researcher Ramiz Gasimov (Daniz)"* with participation of scientists, educational employees and the general public in the society of "Education" in 2002. Full member of ANAS, Academician Magsud Aliyev, full member of ANAS, Academician Jalal Allahverdiyev, corresponding member of ANAS, Professor Ramiz Mammadov, corresponding member of ANAS, Professor Eybali Mehraliyev, Professor Ajdar Agayev, Doctor of pedagogical sciences Afat Bakikhanova and Ganira Amirjanova made speeches at the conference and spoke about the essence of the work.

According to the appeal of the conference's participants, Ramiz Daniz's proofs declaring that, Chhristopher Columbus had used the coordinate system and map of Nasiraddin Tusi when he discovered America are especially interesting. The author has proved that, owing to Tusi, Columbus was aware of existence of America before his transatlantic travel.

"Expedition to India discovers Brazil" may be considered continuation of the author's work started in the field of the history of geographical discoveries and proofs listed in that work are convenient source for scientists working in the mentioned field. The author has described most historical events and important expeditions of the most popular sea travelers, mentioned personal ambitions of some sea travelers, and described division of the world between two kingdoms (Spain and Portugal) primitively by Popes, who considered principles of the church the most important factors of the world. According to the author's investigation, Brazil was discovered in 1494 and I'm sure that, this information will attract attention of scientists.

Number of books written on this theme proves that, this problem is still urgent. Spaniards couldn't know exactly if Portuguese had swindled them with participation of the Pope when the treaty of Tordesillas was concluded in 1494 or Brazil became in the east of the demarcation line by accident. It is interesting that, R. Deniz has elucidated this problem and tried to prove that, representtatives of Portugal had swindled Spaniards by means of the Pope and appropriated Brazil by ruse.

First of all, scientists of Spain, Portugal, Brazil and other countries located on coasts of the Atlantic Ocean will declare their opinions about works of Ramiz Daniz.

Doctor of technical sciences Nugay Aliyev
Chairman of the administrative board of
the society of "Education"

Review - 2

"Expedition to India discovers Brazil" is about the age full of interesting, contradictious problems and obscurities – the beginning of the age of great geographical discoveries (XV-XVII centuries). There was very intensive conflict between great sea countries (Spain, Portugal, Holland, France, England etc.) for hegemony in the Atlantic and Indian Oceans. Expeditions were sent to almost all parts of the Earth for the purpose to pass ahead of opponent countries and to discover new lands.

Discovery of the way to America and Africa, colonization of new lands, increase of exchange of raw materials and goods supported development of the trade, navigation and manufacture and made metropolises rich. That's why rich wealth of India and Chine attracted Europeans.

Early and middle ages (IX-XVI centuries) are the ages of decline of the science and authority of religious thoughts. But, in spite of it, geographical discoveries continued to be made. At the result of efforts of travelers and scientists, geographical descriptions, schemas and maps of discovered lands were prepared. Development of new firm vessels, preparation of sea maps and invention of navigation devices (globe, astrolabe, compass etc.) allowed seamen organize travels to more distant territories. The Greek scientist Claudius Ptolemaeus (II century BC) had stimulated development of the science. He had noted fields of the geography, explained ways of preparation of maps, descrybed cartographic projections in his work **"Geography"** consisting of 8 books and emphasized that the geography consisted of two parts – cartography and regional ethnography. He had fixed coordinates of about 8 thousand settlements and territories in other books. One of them is the map of all known territories. Larger territories of Africa and Asia have been described and coasts have been drawn more precisely on the map of Ptolemaeus than the map of Eratosthenes. Curvature of the Earth has been considered and degrees have been fixed on Ptolemaeus's map.

The geography was developing in Arabian countries as well and broad information was collected about different countries at the result of travels. Travels were carried out by Ubeyd Ibn Shargiyya lived in VII century, Ibn Ruslan, Al-Masudi lived in IX-X centuries and Ibn Battuta lived in the middle of XIV century. The Arabian traveler Al-Masudi had written a book about the nature, history and nations of Front Asia, Central Asia, Caucasus, East Africa, Indonesia and Chine in XX century. He believed that, there was relation between the Indian and Atlantic Oceans. Ibn Battuta from Morocco had passed the Sahara

Desert twice, had reached to eastern coasts of Africa and sailed to Bulgaria along the Volga. He had been in Front Asia, Central Asia, India, Hind-Chine and Chine. In 1498, when Vasco da Gama visited these territories, Arabians had broad trade relations with Hind-Chine and Chine.

Thus, according to historical sources, in the Middle Ages Europeans were sure that, there wasn't a long distance between Europe and India, that's why travelling through the Atlantic Ocean is real.

Renaissance began in Europe in XV century. It became necessary to discover and learn new lands and to collect wealth. But travelling to those countries on land would take a lot of time and ways were dangerous. European countries developed speedily and main purpose was to open seaways.

The first travel of Christopher Columbus stimulated next events and Portuguese started travels towards Brazilian coasts. The Portugal king decided to send secret expedition after Columbus's travel.

Europe was sure that there was large land area — islands in the west of the Atlantic Ocean. But the distance between that land area and Europe was unknown. Portuguese had organized travels towards the west from Madeira Islands, Azores and Green Cape Islands in the middle of XV century.

The author has written that, the reason of the failure of van Olmen and other Portuguese seamen might be as following: they had started their travel in inconvenient period of the year, hadn't prepared well and hadn't used Passats properly unlike Columbus.

The Portuguese seaman Vasco da Gama passed south of Africa and discovered seaway to India in 1498. Form and area of Africa was determined during the travel.

R. Daniz has written that, the history of geographical discoveries had met with new venture at the end of XV century. The expedition saw the coast of Brazil under the leadership of Pedro Alvaresh Cabral on April 22, 1500 and thus, Brazil was discovered officially. But that discovery remained in the history as "the discovery made by accident".

According to the writer and researcher Ramiz Daniz, large land area discovered by Cabral in the western coast of the Atlantic Ocean wasn't discovered by accident and it was the greatest lie of the Portugal kingdom told in XV century. It was impossible to lose way in the ocean, to sail thousands of kilometers blindfold with that expedition's staff, experienced navigators and captains.

The author has noted that, even the most famous scientists of history accepted important geographical discoveries without investigating some events concerning concrete discovery and such discoveries went down in history as "casual discoveries". "Casual" discovery of Brazil is obvious case of it.

According to results achieved by Ramiz Daniz, Cabral's expedition fulfilled the secret task of the king Manuel I. The staff of the expedition had to prove existence of lands, which located on western coasts of the Atlantic Ocean, were known by Portuguese and was secret for the world community.

According to historical sources, participant of Cabral's expedition – Duarte Pereira had been in lands located on the other side of the Atlantic Ocean. Pereira reached Brazilian coasts in 1494 for the first time in accordance with the secret task. Author's investigations also proved it. Thus, Pereira could reach Brazilian coasts six years before Cabral and knew the way to that territory.

Duarte Pereira drew outlines of the coast line and determined its coordinates when reached Brazilian coasts. But as the seaman hurried to fulfill the king's task, he couldn't check the coast line and thought that the territory he discovered is an island, but not a continent. P.

Cabral repeated that mistake after six years. Though Portuguese achieved their goals, they couldn't even imagine that, the territory they had discovered was a continent.

Portuguese, who had enough necessary information, demanded to move the demarcation line towards 50^0 west longitude in order to ensure fair division as if they didn't know anything about existence of Brazil. Representatives of Spaniards were sure that, Portuguese, who weren't aware of existence of western lands, wanted to own some additional water basin in the ocean. They didn't object to compromising useless ocean waters to Portuguese in order to avoid superfluous conflict. Portuguese had the luck and Columbus's first travel was helpful for them. Only ocean waters had been drawn at 65^0-70^0 west longitude in his report.

According to the treaty of Tordesillas concluded in 1494, the demarcation line was moved for 370 liq – 46^0 $30^/$ towards the west from Azores and Brazil became property of Portugal. Thus, Portuguese swindled Spaniards by means of the Pope Alexander Borgia VI and appropriated Brazil.

The author has noted that, such unjust division disclaimed efforts of Spaniards. Nevertheless, Spaniards should be known as authors of the mentioned discovery as Brazilian coasts were visited by Spanish sea travelers Vicente Pinson and Diego Lepe for the first time (January and February of 1500).

Illustrations (pictures, map-schemas, demarcation line on the map, images of ancient and new maps and globes) are also one of positive features of the work. Those illustrations attract attention of readers and are very interesting.

The writer and researcher Ramiz Daniz has analyzed the history of geographical discoveries, knowledge got at the result of sea travels, activities of remarkable sea travelers and development of the science and cartography. The author has noted that, America had been described on the globe made by Martin Behaim (1492) and he has included the globe's image in the book.

The Florentine scientist Paolo Toscanelli gained great fame in Europe for his well-known world map made in 1474. Toscanelli had told the Portugal king Alfonso V that, the Earth was spherical and it was possible to sail to India through the west. Ramiz Daniz has written following thought at the result of his investigations: Columbus had prepared his transatlantic project by means of the astronomic catalogue **"Zij-i-Ilkhani"** prepared by Nasiraddin Tusi, but not in accordance with the map made by Paolo Toscanelli.

Because of the struggle existing in the second half of XV century between Spain and Portugal for division of the world, most expeditions of that time fulfilled secret tasks. That's why names of authors of some important discoveries kept secret. So the book **"Expedition to India discovers Brazil"** is very significant for answering the question "Who has discovered Brazil".

Ramiz Daniz has tried to elucidate obscurities of the complicated history and contradictious events of XV century. He has achieved this goal after learning historical sources and chronology. The author has described new thoughts and results after analyzing the chronology of the age of great geographical discoveries. He has decidedly investigated very complicated and interesting period of the history. There are too many information (historical personalities, events, well-known scientists, discoveries, new continents and territories, division of the world, development of navigation, geography and cartography, contradictory hypothesizes of scientists) concerning that period. The research work has been written by using interesting and rich historical and geographical information.

To our mind, **"Expedition to India discovers Brazil"** written by the writer and researcher Ramiz Daniz is a successful work, which will rouse great interest in readers. We wish greater successes to the author!

Ramiz Mammadov – Laureate of State Prize
Associate Member of the Academy of Science,
doctor of technical sciences, director of the Institute
of Geography of the Academy of Science

Candidate of geographical sciences
Shamil Azizov

Literature

1. Абрамсон, М. Л. Кириллова, А. А. Колесницкий Н. Ф. и др.; Под ред. Колесницкого Н.Ф. История

средних веков: 2-е изд. испр. и доп. Москва, «Просвещение», 1986.

2. Авадяева Е. Н., Зданович Л. И. Сто великих мореплавателей. Москва, «Вече», 1999.

3. Андре М. Подлинное приключение Христофора Колумба. Пер. с фран. М-Л., Земля и фабрика, 1928.

4. Атлас истории географических открытий и исследований. М., «Главное управление геодезий и карт». 1959.

5. Azərbaycan Beynəlxalq Universiteti. N.Tusinin 800 illik yubileyinə həsr edilmiş Respublika konfransının material-ları. Bakı-2001

6. Афанасьев. В. Л. Текст воспроизведен по изданию: Бартоломе де Лас Касас. История Индии. Ленинград, «Наука», 1968.

7. Белый Ю. А. Тихо Браге. М. «Наука», 1982.

8. Бейкер Дж. История географических открытий и исследований. пер. с англ. Москва, «Издательство иностранной литературы»., 1950.

9. Бейкер Дж. История географических открытий и исследований. Перевод с англ. под редакцией и с предисловием Магидовича И. П. М., «Издательство иностранной литературы». 1950.

10. Бейклесс Дж. Америка глазами первооткрывателей. Пер. с англ. М., «Прогресс», 1969.

11. Блон Жорж. Атлантический океан.

12. Бушков А.А. Статья - Кем был Христофор Колумб и он ли открыл Америку? Из книги «Россия, которой не было: загадки, версии, гипотезы», 1998. Тайны истории. Онлайн архив.

13. Верлинден Ч. Христофор Колумб, Эрнан Кортес. Ростов-на-Дону, «Феникс», 1997.

14. Верн Ж. Открытие Земли. Москва. Издательство «АСТ», 2012.

15. Вязов Е. И. Васко да Гама. М., «Географгиз», 1956.

16. Голант В. Я. Планету открывали сообща. М., «Наука», 1971.

17. Гордеева З. И. История географических открытий. Учебное пособие для вузов. Москва, «Юрайт», 2019.

18. Гуляев В. И. Доколумбовы плавания в Америку: мифы и реальность. Москва, «Международные отношения», 1991.

19. Гумилевская М. А. Как открывали мир. Москва, «Д.Л.», 1997.

20. Qacar Ç. Azərbaycanın görkəmli şəxsiyyətləri. Bakı, "Nicat", 1997.

21. Qasımov R. Əsrləri qabaqlamış alim – Nəsirəddin Tusi. Bakı, "Yurd", 2003. səh. 267.

22. Qasımov R. Xristofor Kolumb, Nəsirəddin Tusi və Amerika qitəsinin həqiqi kəşfi. Bakı, "Çaşıoğlu", 2002.

23. Daniz R. Amerigo Vespucci, Martin Waldsemuller - secret bargain. "Lap Lambert Academic Publishing", Riga. 2019.

24. Daniz R. Christopher Columbus, Nasiraddin Tusi and real discovery of America. "Lap Lambert Academic Publishing", Riga. 2019.

25. Daniz R. The scientist passed ahead of centuries – Nasiraddin Tusi. "Lap Lambert Academic Publishing", Riga. 2019.

26. Джейн К. Г. Васко да Гама и его преемники (1460-1580).

27. Дживелегов А. К. Текст печатается по изданию: Леонардо да Винчи. Избранные произведения: в 2 т. - М.; Л.: Academia, 1935. (Искусствоведение). Москва. Издательство «Студии Артемия Лебедева». 2010.

28. Дитмар А. Б. Родосская параллель. Жизнь и деятельность Эратосфена. Москва, «Мысль», 1965.

29. Ибаньес /Бласко Ибаньес/ В. В поисках великого хана. Калининград, 1987. С. 532 и ел.

30. Источник: https://podparusami.club/a-zemlya-pravda-kruglaya-chto-otkryl-miru-magellan-v-pervom-krugosvetnom-puteshestvii/

31. Hüseynov R. Ə. "Bilgi" dərgisinin "fizika, riyaziyyat, yer elmləri" seriyası. Nəsirəddin Tusinin astronomiya elmində xidmətləri. Bakı, 2002, №2.

32. Ионина Н. А. Автор-составитель. Сто великих чудес света. Москва, «Вече», 2000.

33. Исаченко А. А. Развитие географических идей. Москва, «Мысль», 1971.

34. Əmrahov M. Böyük ipək yolu. Bakı, "Mütərcim", 2011. səh. 52.

35. Константинова Н. С. Путешествие в прошлое. Навигационная ошибка или секретная миссия? «Латинская Америка», № 5, М.2000, С.8.

36. Колумб Х. Путешествие. Москва, 1952.

37. Коротцев О. Как измеряли мир. Глобус. Л., «Д.Л», 1980.

38. Купер Ф. Дж. Мерседес из Кастилии или путешествие в Катай. Одесса, «Маяк», 1985.

39. Las Casas B.de. Historia de las Indias. Mexico, 1951. T. I. P. 118.

40. Лас Касас Б. История Индий. Пр. с исп. Л., «Наука», 1968.

41. Лас Касас, Б. де. История Индий. Книга вторая. Глава 8. https://www.indiansworld.org/kniga-vtoraya-glava-6-glava-15.html#.Xr6qn_8zbIV.

42. Лас Касас, Б. де. История Индий. Книга вторая. Глава 8. https://www.indiansworld.org/kniga-vtoraya-glava-6-glava-15.html#.Xr6qn_8zbIV.

43. Ле Пти Фюте. Путеводитель «Бразилия». Москва, 1997 г.

44. Лиелас А. Каравеллы выходят в океан. Пер. с латыш. Рига, «Лиесма», 1969.

45 Магидович И. П. Христофор Колумб. Москва, «Географгиз», 1956.

46. Магидович И. П. История открытия и исследования Центральной и Южной Америки. М., «Мысль», 1965.

47. Магидович И. П., Магидович В. И. Очерки по истории географических открытий. I Том. Москва, «Просвещение», 1982.

48. Магидович И. П, Магидович В. И. Очерки по истории географических открытий. II Том. Москва, «Просвещение», 1982.

49. Максудов Ф. Г., Маммедбейли Г. Дж. Мухаммед Насирэддин Туси. Баку, «Гянджилик», 1981.

50. Малухин С.С. Журнал «Самиздат» - история индейцев Америки.

http://samlib.ru/m/maluhin_s_s/samizdat-istoriaindeicevameriki.shtml 01.01. 2014.

51. Марко Поло. Книга Марко Поло. Пер. старофранцузского текста. Москва, «Мысль», 1965.

52. Мирошников В. В., Мирошникова В. В. Скляренко В. М. Знаменитые путешественники. Издательство: Фолио, 2014 г.

Подробнее: https://www.labirint.ru/books/462087/

53. Морисон С. Э. Христофор Колумб мореплаватель. Перевод с англ. М., «Издательство иностранной литературы». 1958.

54. Муромов И. А. Сто великих путешественников. Москва, «Вече», 2000.

55. Məmmədbəyli H. C. Mühəmməd Nəsirəddin Tusi. Bakı, "Gənclik", 1980.

56. Müdərris Rüzavi M. T. Əhval və asar-e Xace Nəsirəddin Tusi. II nəşr. Tehran, "Gülşən", 1991.

57. Непомнящий Н.Н., Жуков А.В. Запрещенная история, или Колумб Америку не открывал. В. © ООО «Издательство Алгоритм», 2013.

58. Окно в мир. Путеводитель «Южная Америка». Москва, 1998 г.

59. Перес Ж. Изабелла католичка. Образец для христианского мира? Санкт-Петербург, из-во «Евразия». 2013.

60. Письма Америго Веспуччи. Перевод с латиньского и итал. «Издательство иностранной литературы». – В сб. Бригантина – 71. М., «Молодая гвардия», 1971.

61. Помбу (Роша-Помбу) Ж. Ф. История Бразилии. Пер. с порт. 7-е изд. М., «Издательство иностранной литературы». 1962.

62. Путешествия Христофора Колумба. Дневники, письма, документы, 4-е издание. М., «Географгиз», 1961.

63. Самин Д. К. Сто великих научных открытий. М, «Вече», 2002.

64. Самин Д. К. Сто великих ученых. Москва, «Вече», 2002.

65. Слёзкин Л. Ю. Земля Святого Креста. Открытие и завоевание Бразилии. М., «Наука». 1970.

66. Свет Я. М. Колумб. М., «Молодая гвардия», 1973.

67. Свет Я. М. Текст воспроизведен по изданию: Путешествия Христофора Колумба. Москва.

68. Свет Я. М. Севильская западня. (Тяжба о Колумбовом наследстве) Москва, «Молодая гвардия», 1969.

69. Стингл М. Индейцы без томагавков. Пер. с чешского В. А. Каменской и О. М. Малевича под редакцией Р. В. Кинжалова. Москва. «Прогресс», 1984.

70. Страбон. География. Пер. с гречес. Москва, «Наука», 1964.

71. Субботин В.А. Великие Открытия. Колумб. Васко да Гама. Магеллан. Журнал «Мир истории», 2000-2003.

72. Хазанов А. Б. Неизвестное о Васко да Гаме. Вопросы истории, 2000, №8.

73. Хазанов А. Б. Секретное открытие Бразилии. «НГ-Наука», №3, 31 марта 2001 г.

74. Ханке Х. Люди, корабли, океаны. Москва, «Прогресс» 1984.

75. Харт Г. Венецианец Марко Поло. Перевод с англ. Москва, «ИЛ», 1956.

76. Хауз. Д. Гринвичское время и открытие долготы. Москва, «Мир», 1983.

77. Хенниг Р. Неведомые земли. Т. 4. М., 1963. стр. 222.

78. Хепгуд Ч. Древние карты морских королей.

79. Христофор Колумб. Путешествие. 1952.

80. Цвейг С. Собрание сочинений в семи томах. Звездные часы человечества. III том. Москва, «Правда», 1963.

81. Цукерник Д. Я. Как была открыта Америка? «Новый мир», 1962, № 12.

82. Шкловский В. Земли разведчик. М., «Молодая гвардия», 1966.

Table of contents

Ramiz Daniz

Expedition to India discovers Brazil

156 p.

Baku – 2022

Computer design: - Sinay Gasimova
Designer: - Sevinj Akchurina
Translator: - Hokume Hebibova

Printed in Great Britain
by Amazon

75522259R00092